Read and Write Sports

Other Recently Published Teacher Ideas Press Titles

Read and Write Sports

Readers Theatre and Writing Activities for Grades 3–8

Anastasia Suen

A Teacher Ideas Press Book

 LIBRARIES UNLIMITED

AN IMPRINT OF ABC-CLIO, LLC
Santa Barbara, California • Denver, Colorado • Oxford, England

Library of Congress Cataloging-in-Publication Data

Suen, Anastasia.
    Read and write sports : readers theatre and writing activities for grades 3-8 / Anastasia Suen.
        p. cm. — (A teacher ideas press book)
    Includes bibliographical references.
    ISBN 978–1–59884–631–7 (hardcopy : alk. paper) — ISBN 978–1–59884–632–4 (ebook)
1. Sports journalism—Juvenile literature. 2. Sportscasters—Juvenile literature. 3. Sportswriters—Juvenile literature. I. Title.
PN4784.S6S94   2011
372.62'3044—dc22   2010051960

ISBN: 978–1–59884–631–7
EISBN: 978–1–59884–632–4   47631964 12/11

15 14 13 12 11   1 2 3 4 5

This book is also available on the World Wide Web as an eBook.
Visit www.abc-clio.com for details.

Libraries Unlimited
An Imprint of ABC-CLIO, LLC

ABC-CLIO, LLC
130 Cremona Drive, P.O. Box 1911
Santa Barbara, California 93116-1911

This book is printed on acid-free paper ∞

Manufactured in the United States of America

All graphic organizers were designed by Aimée Suen.

For Aimée and Shirley

Contents

Acknowledgments

I want to thank all of the schools and libraries in Texas Education Service Center Regions 10 and 11 who invited me to work with their young writers in the Allen ISD, Carrollton-Farmers Branch ISD, Coppell ISD, Dallas ISD, Diocese of Dallas Schools, Duncanville ISD, Fort Worth ISD, Frisco ISD, Keller ISD, Krum ISD, Garland ISD, Highland Park ISD, Irving ISD, Lewisville ISD, Lewisville Public Library, Mesquite ISD, Plano ISD, Plano Public Library, Richardson ISD, and the Richardson Public Library and the Van Alstyne Public Library.

With special thanks to Susan Allison, Dr. Lea Bailey, Julie Briggs, Teena Garvin, Lisa Haliburton, Leigh Ann Jones, Diane Lutz, Tish Mulkey, Cindy Nietubicz, Dorette Putonti, Dr. Christopher Salerno, Karen Shull, and Mary Woodard.

Introduction

Reading and Writing . . . and Teaching

My mother read to me as a child, so books have always been a part of my life. I wrote and illustrated my first picture book when I was 11 years old, and I've been writing ever since. I wrote as a student and I wrote as a teacher. After all, I was charged with teaching my students how to read and write. I read to them and wrote for them, and they read and wrote for me. I wrote easy readers for my kindergarten and first grade students. When I taught the intermediate grades, I wrote plays for my students to perform.

After my children were born, I began to send my writing to book publishers, and to my dismay, received rejection letters for years. When my youngest was in second grade, I finally sold my first book. (Six weeks later I sold my second book and six weeks after that I sold my third book. After all those years of hearing no, someone finally said yes!)

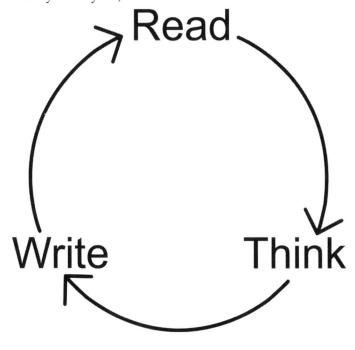

During all this time, I was writing and teaching. For me, *writing and teaching go hand-in-hand. They are yin and yang.* I need to be quiet to hear my thoughts so I can write them down. And yet when I talk about my thoughts with others, what I want to say becomes clearer.

Communication is an ever widening spiral. I read something, and that makes me think, which leads me to write. Reading what I have written leads to new thoughts, so I write again. As I cycle through the creative process this way, my thoughts become clearer and clearer.

I discovered that writing is actually the final step of the creative process. Without previous experiences, I really didn't have anything to write about. That was why I got stuck! I need to read and think and *live* before I can write about something. *A lack of experience is the first source of writer's block.*

I brought my personal experience with writer's block into the classroom. I only ask students to write about something that they know or want to find out. Student-directed learning is motivated learning.

Another thing I discovered over the years is that the writing process is easier when I have a map. Sitting at a desk with a blank page is terrifying! How do I know where the story should go? What should I do? I know I'm not alone in this. I see it in every classroom I work in (and I have taught kindergarten to college). *A lack of direction is the second source of writer's block.*

When I share my fear of the blank page with students, it always lowers the tension. They realize they are not alone, and become open to writing and thinking and sharing. I share my maps with them, and guide them through the creative process. As we talk through their story, students of all ages are always amazed at how the words come pouring out. I tell them that their words are already there, we just need to use a map to find them. We just need to ask the right questions.

Peer Editing

As you share this question-directed writing process with your students, you are also teaching your students to be editors. Yes, even elementary school students can help each other write. Peer editing is an important part of becoming a writer. Asking questions at each stage of the writing process helps young writers clarify what they want to say. It is a practical way to help your students realize that they are writing for an audience.

Using peer editors also helps you individualize your instruction. Your active learners are helping each other, giving you time to work with other students one-on-one. Everyone is learning. It's a win-win!

You are holding a book of writing maps in your hand. Today we call these writing maps Graphic Organizer Charts (GO Charts). With these maps, you can help your students discover the stories they have inside. They will help your students discover stories in the world around them. These Graphic Organizer Charts will guide your students on their journey as readers, thinkers, and writers. They will give you questions to ask your students, so they can discover their stories step-by-step.

In the classroom, I found that students had an easier time using the maps when they saw how someone else had used them, so the GO Charts in this book appear in two different forms. In the sports chapters, you will find completed examples of each GO Chart. At the back of the book, there are black line masters of each GO Chart for you to reproduce. After you model how another student created the sample GO Chart, you can hand out copies of the black line masters for your students to use.

Prewriting, the Forgotten Step

There are writing charts in classrooms all over the country that show the five steps of writing.

The Five Steps of Writing

1. Prewrite
2. Rough Draft
3. Revise
4. Edit
5. Publish

Younger students skip the first step. Young writers simply don't plan ahead. They get an idea and they write it down. This is developmentally appropriate in the primary grades.

As students grow older, however, we want to help them learn how to think ahead. We want them to learn how to plan. However, because they have been writing for several years without this step, many writers see it as unnecessary.

I'll be honest and tell you that I see this with many adult writers that I work with as well. Some writers don't plan ahead; they just sit down and write. The problem comes later when they are halfway through their novel and don't know what to do next. Any editing I try to do is met with resistance. They have spent months working on those chapters! Who am I to tell them that those chapters are unnecessary and need to be deleted? They don't want me to touch their precious words, because they think they are done. (They don't really want critique, they want praise. In their minds, what they have written is golden.)

This is why I like to work with the maps first. If I can help them to plan their story before they spend a lot of time on it, students of all ages are much more open to the editing process. The GO Charts are filled in with just a few words and phrases, so the work is finished quickly. Because they haven't spent hours working on these words, most students are quite open to discussing changes. After all, how hard is it to cross off a few words on the page? So they cross off a few words here and add a few others there. And then we talk about it and they do it again. Their first idea isn't always the best one. Sometimes it takes a few tries to figure things out. I have found that helping students be open to change at this early stage results in stronger and more focused writing in the end. Editing in the prewriting stage makes the writing process a lot less traumatic for everyone.

Why Sports?

I selected sports as the topic of this writing book because in classroom after classroom, it was the only topic that many students want to write about. Once I told them they could write about their favorite sports, my "reluctant" writers became "active" writers. They wanted to tell me all about their favorite sport and what they did at their last game.

To capitalize on this strong interest, I have selected 10 sports.

1. Football
2. Basketball
3. Hockey
4. Skating
5. Baseball
6. Soccer
7. Track
8. Gymnastics
9. BMX
10. Skateboarding

These sports are listed in the order they usually occur during the school year. This will allow you to use this book with your class throughout the year.

How to Use This Book

For each of the 10 sports in this volume, your students will read, write, and work with words. In each chapter, there is a readers theatre selection, an expository writing exercise, a narrative writing exercise, a poetry writing exercise, and two word puzzles. The lesson plans are here in this section. The student pages include a readers theatre script, example GO Charts for each sport, and the two word puzzles. The GO Chart masters are in Appendix One and the puzzle solutions are in Appendix Two.

Readers Theatre

Each readers theatre script has an introduction page with a summary of the play, the reading level, staging directions and props suggestions. To allow you to cast the play accurately, the reading level for each speaking part is also listed on the teacher's summary page. Dialogue is short, so the reading levels for most of the speaking parts are quite low. This will allow your "reluctant" readers to stand in front of the class and read with confidence. Every play also has a chorus speaking part for the "crowd" or the "fans" so the entire class will be able to participate (which will keep everyone on task).

Ask students to write their name at the top of their script. They should also highlight their lines part with a marker. Because each student is part of the play, they will have to read along each time it is performed. The highlighted sections will remind students when it is their turn to speak.

A readers theatre play is not the same as a traditional school play.

Traditional school play	Readers Theatre
• students recite their lines from memory	• students read from a script
• the play is held onstage	• the play takes place in the classroom
• students dress in costumes	• no costumes are required
• a backdrop and props are always used	• backdrop and props are optional

The goal of any readers theatre performance is to give students practice reading aloud. This is accomplished in two ways. As students prepare for the performance, they read the play over and over. During the performance they read the words again aloud.

Write an Expository Paragraph

We will begin our writing in each chapter with the facts. This will ground your students in the world of each sport. (It's hard to write about something you don't understand.)

Each student will write an expository paragraph about one aspect of the sport. The paragraph will answer a student-directed question. As you can see in the chart, there are five different steps. Selecting a topic is always a difficult task for some students. In each chapter that task will be made somewhat easier by the fact that we are focusing on only one sport. For avid fans, however, there are still too many choices, so we'll use a mind map to narrow things down. Let's use the baseball chapter as an example.

So students can see their tasks at a glance, make a copy of this Write an Expository Paragraph Chart, found in Appendix One, for each student's writing folder. The black line masters for the Topic GO Charts are in the appendix after this instruction chart.

Name_____ Date_____

Write an Expository Paragraph Chart

1. Select a topic.

2. Think of a question.

3. Find 5 facts that answer your question.

4. Organize your facts.

5. Write about your facts.

Warm-Up

Every sport begins with a warm-up, so for our sports writing, we will warm up too! For expository writing, we will begin with the Topic Mind Map GO Chart.

Hand out copies of the completed Baseball Topic Mind Map GO Chart. Point out that the name of the sport is written in the center of the chart. The other words on the chart are all related to the word in the center. Ask students to read the words aloud.

Draw your students' attention to the question at the bottom of the chart. Tell them that the student who created this chart wanted to know more about this aspect of baseball.

After discussing the completed example, hand out blank Topic Mind Map GO Charts for the students to use. Ask them to write the name of the sport in the center circle and create their own mind map. (Some of your lower-level students will still find this task difficult, so tell them that they can use these words from the example on their mind map, too.)

After each student has a completed mind map, the next step is to think of a question. When they look at these words, what do they want to know? What do they want to find out? Ask students to write their question at the bottom of their chart.

Name Abigail   Date January 9

Baseball Topic Mind Map GO Chart

Write the name of your sport in the center circle and add details in the smaller circles. This brainstorming will help you figure out a research question. What do you want to know about this sport?

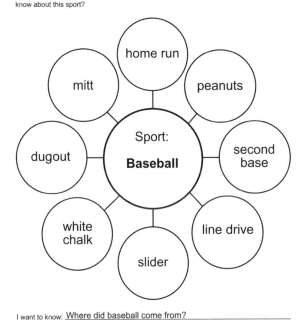

I want to know: Where did baseball come from?

Regulations

Now that everyone is warmed up, it is time to talk about the rules of the game. Before your students begin their research, you need to give them clear guidelines.

Hand out the example Baseball Topic ISP GO Chart. Ask students to read the baseball question at the top of the chart.

If you have not already used an ISP chart with your class, you will need to introduce this concept. When researching, we need to know three things:

1. I is the information
2. S is the source
3. P is the page

Take a minute to talk about the triangle at the top of the chart. The triangle is there to remind students to find information from three different sources. Triangulation is a tool nonfiction writers use to determine the accuracy of their information. If information is not "backed up" by two other sources, it may not be accurate and should not be reported as fact. Information that can not be verified is hearsay. (Before this lesson, decide if you will allow hearsay to be reported as such, or will only allow verified facts.)

The goal of this writing exercise is to find enough information for students to write a paragraph that answers their sports question. Repeat this goal as you introduce this new GO Chart. (It is very easy to get lost in a deluge of information, so remembering the goal will help your students focus on the task at hand.)

As you look over the completed chart with the students, point out the short phrases used to record information. Note taking doesn't mean copying, it means writing the facts briefly in your own words. Use key words and phrases, not complete sentences.

Name Abigail   Date January 9

Baseball Topic ISP GO Chart

Find the answer to your sports research question with this ISP chart. Use short phrases to record your Information, Source, and Page.

I want to know: Where did baseball come from?

I: think it came from a game called rounders
S: Library of Congress
P: http://www.americaslibrary.gov/cgi-bin/page.cgi/jp/bball/early_1

I: the bases in rounders are poles (1760 book)
S: Library of Congress
P: http://www.americaslibrary.gov/jp/bball/jp_bball_early_1_e.html

I: baseball like rounders but not the same
S: baseball history webpage
P: http://www.solarnavigator.net/sport/baseball.htm

I: rounders has 4 bases and "home"
S: Rounder's League page
P: http://buryrounders.org.uk/thegame.htm

I: to score, you hit the ball with a bat and run around the 4 bases
S: Cornwall sports league
P: http://www.cornwallsportspartnership.co.uk/sports/rounders

---

Note Taking Mini-lesson

If note taking is a new skill for your students, before the lesson, bookmark the webpages used in the Topic ISP GO Chart and retrace the steps. Ask the students to read the sources and to see how little was written on the GO Chart. Point out the use of key words and phrases. (Each Topic ISP GO Chart will use internet sources so you can repeat this mini-lesson for each sport. Use the online databases at your school or public library.)

The Game

Depending on your school's resources, your students can research their questions in/with

- the classroom library
- your school library
- your classroom computers
- the library or learning lab computers
- their home computers

When your students have completed their own Topic ISP GO Charts, ask them to take out their copy of the Baseball Topic ISP GO Chart. Now we will use the Topic ISP GO Chart for a second purpose, to *organize* the facts.

If your students were going to write the paragraph for the example Topic ISP GO Chart, which detail would they use first after the topic/question? Have them write a 1 in front of that detail. Now what comes second, third, fourth, and last? Have them write the numbers for these details as well.

Now hand out copies of the example Baseball Topic Sandwich GO Chart. Did your students make the same decisions that this student did?

You may find that some students have organized the material in a different way. If the information is organized in a clear and logical manner, then the student has accomplished this task successfully. If not, then the student will need to reorganize his or her information so that the person reading the paragraph understands what the student is trying to say.

It's time for your students to organize their own facts. Which detail comes first, second, third, fourth, and last? Ask students to write a number in front of each detail. Then they can swap papers and talk their decisions over with their peer editor.

After the organizing step has been edited, students can fill out their own Topic Sandwich GO Chart. They will copy their question/topic and all 5 details in order.

The completed Baseball Topic Sandwich GO Chart has one extra item, a conclusion. After asking a question and finding information from three different sources, we want students to come to a conclusion. In other words, we want them to answer their original question. The answer to their question is the logical ending of this paragraph.

Writing a conclusion is the final prewriting step. Then students can meet with their peer editors again. This will them help clarify what they have written. When this round of editing is completed, the students are ready to write their paragraph. Remind them to use full sentences as they explain their facts in detail using their own words.

Name Abigail   Date January 9

Baseball Topic Sandwich GO Chart

Organize the information from your ISP chart so you can write your sports paragraph.

Question/Topic: Where did baseball come from?

Detail: think it came from a game called rounders

Detail: to score, you hit the ball with a bat and run around 4 bases

Detail: rounders has 4 bases and "home"

Detail: the bases in rounders are poles (1760 book)

Detail: baseball like rounders but not the same

Conclusion: baseball probably came from game rounders

Write a Narrative Scene

After exploring the facts, it's time to share stories. For active participants in each sport, these writing exercises may be written as personal narratives. For other students, it will be pure fiction. (And some will combine both—no one remembers everything and life goes on and on while a story has a beginning, middle, and end.)

Each student will write a short scene. A scene is not the story of the entire game. A scene is a small part of a longer story, and it is over in a matter of minutes. This makes the task more manageable for classroom writing.

Name_____ Date_____

Write a Narrative Scene Chart

1. Make a mind map.

2. Think threes (a person in a place with a problem).

3. Make an action list.

4. Add details.

5. Write your scene.

You may decide to allow your more fluent writers to write several scenes. A chapter in a middle grade novel often has three to five scenes. A chapter is not the entire story, but it does have a beginning, middle, and end. At the beginning of a chapter the main character wants something and feels a certain way, but by the end of that chapter what the character wants and/or how he or she feels has changed.

In many of the examples in this book I have modeled the longer three- to five-scene version. If your students are active participants in the selected sport, they will find it easy to write about it at length. (In fact, they may have trouble limiting themselves to just a few scenes. Some students will want to give you a play-by-play recap of the entire game.) For non-players, however, writing a single scene might be a challenge. You may need to have novels about each sport in your classroom library for any non-players. Students can also view sports clip videos online.

Once again, we will begin with a brainstorming step. This will help students think about which aspect of the sport they would like to write about. What will happen in their scene? The mind map will help them make a choice.

A copy of this Write a Narrative Scene Chart can be found in the Appendix One with the black line masters for this section. Make a copy for each student's writing folder.

Warm-Up

Hand out copies of the completed Baseball Scene Mind Map GO Chart. Point out that the name of the sport is written in the center of the chart. The other words on the chart are all things that happen during this sport. It is not a list of words but rather a list of possible scenes. Ask students to read the scenes aloud.

The student who created this chart wrote down several possible scenes that happened when this sport is played. After thinking about these scenes, the student made a decision. That decision is recorded at the bottom of the chart in the "I want to write about" line.

Now it's time for your students to write. After discussing the completed example, hand out blank Scene Mind Map GO Charts for the students to use. Ask them to write the name of the sport in the center circle and create their own mind map.

When each student has a completed mind map, the next step is to make the decision. Which scenes do they want to write about? Ask students to write their decision at the bottom of their chart.

Name Joseph   Date January 11

Baseball Scene Mind Map GO Chart

A scene is a small part of a longer story. It is over in a matter of minutes. What can happen in just a few minutes when you play this sport? Write the sport in the center circle and add details in the smaller circles. This will help you decide what aspect of this sport you can write about today.

crossing home plate

stealing a base

tagging a runner

catching a ball

Sport: **Baseball**

hitting a line drive

hitting a foul ball

making a slider

batting

I want to write about: batting

Regulations

Your students have warmed up, so it's time to explain the rules of the game. Give each student a copy of the example Baseball Scene Threes GO Chart. Now that they have decided which scene they will write, it's time to add more specifics.

Name **Joseph**   Date **January 11**

Baseball Scene Threes GO Chart

Real life goes on and on but a story starts when something changes. Your readers want to find out how someone solves a problem. Where is that person and what is the problem? Decide on the 3 essential elements of your scene. Use short phrases to record your decisions.

I want to write about: **batting**

To write a scene, you need 3 things:

a **PERSON:** number 7 on the Orioles

in a **PLACE:** at a home plate in a baseball game

with a **PROBLEM:** going to bat to try and hit the ball

PERSON: Who will play baseball in their scene?

Will the student play, or will he or she write about someone else? That choice will determine the voice used in the scene. Most students write personal narratives in first person, using the "I" voice. Stories about another person are usually written in third person, the "he or she" voice.

PLACE: Where will the person be in this scene?

A scene takes place in one specific location. Where will your character be?

PROBLEM: What is the person trying to do in this scene?

Each player in the game has a job to do, so we need to know what that job is. In this example scene the player is up at bat. His job is to walk up to home plate, hit the ball, and run to first base.

Before students complete their own chart, remind them that they are only writing a scene, not the entire game. *What will happen in the next few minutes?* (The Scene Threes GO Chart black line masters are in Appendix One.)

Ask students to share their completed chart with a peer editor. When everyone has "a person in a place with a problem," it's time to expand that into a list of specific actions. Give each student a copy of the example Baseball Scene Story Boxes GO Chart.

The main character's actions are the focus of the story boxes chart. What the other players say and do will be added later. Remind students that this is just a planning chart. The chart is not for writing sentences. All they need to write is a short action phrase.

After reviewing the example Story Boxes GO Chart, ask students to fill out one of their own. The master Story Boxes GO Chart has instructions at the top and at the bottom. For Step 1, they only need to follow the directions at the top of the chart. The directions at the bottom are for Step 2.

As students complete Step 1 and make a list of actions for their scene, ask them to consult with you or a peer editor. Their peer editor will read over the ideas and see if they make any sense. *It's much easier to edit at the prewriting stage, when there are just a few words on the page.* I find that students (from elementary school to college) are much more open to editing short phrases. Finding gaps or flaws at this prewriting stage saves a lot of time and heartache later. It also creates the awareness of writing for an audience.

Name Joseph   Date January 11

Baseball Scene Story Boxes (Step 1) GO Chart

Step 1: What happens during your scene? Write a short action phrase in each box.

- walks to home plate
- swings the bat
- swings the bat
- hits the ball
- runs to first base

Name Joseph   Date January 11

Baseball Scene Story Boxes (Step 2) GO Chart

Step 1: What happens during your scene? Write a short action phrase in each box.

-#7 on the Orioles / wants to get a hit	walks to home plate	raises the bat / hoping for a good pitch
looks at the pitcher's shirt / Badgers' pitcher winds up	swings the bat	the ball comes / surprised it was a miss
looks at grass in outfield / the pitcher winds up	swings the bat	the ball comes / upset at second miss
the pitcher winds up / loud sound when bat hits	hits the ball	crowd yells / ball goes to left field
drops bat on ground / touches first base	runs to first base	makes it in time / happy

Step 2: Add 4 details (actions, descriptions, feelings) to each box.

The Game

Now that students have a basic outline of what happens during their scene, they can add details for Step 2.

For Step 2 there are four lines coming out of each box, two on the left and two on the right. The purpose of these lines is to remind students that they need to add specific details to each and every part of their scene.

Before students work on their own, look at the Step 2 example GO Chart again and talk about the type of details they can add. Actions are important in sports, but for our readers we also need to add descriptions and emotions. How a character feels is an important part of a scene, and one that students often forget.

Name_____ Date_____

Feelings Chart

How does the person feel?

Sad	Happy	Angry
Hurt	Excited	Worried
Bored	Embarrassed	Tired

© Anastasia Suen, 2010

Name_____ Date_____

Five Senses Chart

Use your five senses:

See   Hear

Touch   Taste

Smell

© Anastasia Suen, 2010

Using the five senses will also bring the scene alive. What did the character see, hear, touch, taste, or smell? Specific details make the story come alive, so that readers feel they are there, inside the story.

A copy of these details charts can be found in Appendix One so you can make a copy for each student to keep in his or her writing folder.

No Erasing Rule

I strongly recommend that you implement a "no erasing" rule for your writing workshops. Ideas take time to develop and working writers often go back to earlier drafts to reuse material. Erasing makes that impossible, and it also leaves the student with nothing to show for his or her time. Writing is a process, not a product. It takes time to clarify your thoughts. Honor the process and insist that all recorded thoughts remain on the page.

A "no erasing" rule will also help you guide your young writers. What students have written on the page will let you know what type of questions you need to ask. Abiding by this rule is especially helpful when students insist that they are "stuck." Ask them to tell you about what they have written, and go from there.

To reinforce this concept, you may wish to teach your students proofreading marks. Professional writers cross out words and use special marks to show the changes they want to make. They don't erase. (This chart can be found in Appendix One. It has a name and date line at the top so you can make a copy for each student's writing folder.)

By adding details to the Story Boxes GO Chart, your students can work from a single document as they create their story. As you move on to Step 2, the "adding details" step, you will have students who want to start over on a new page because their work is too messy, or because they have changed their mind about their story. (Yes, some students want to write a completely new story!)

I always stop at this point and talk a bit about the writing process. Writing is not a linear process, it is a creative one, and that means that sometimes things just don't work out. If you need to start over, then you need to start over. (It's far better to find out in the prewriting stage that a story isn't working than to find out after you have spent hours working on it!)

What this means is that from this point on you will have students working at various stages, depending on both their stage as a writer and the stage that their story is in. (As students work on their own they can refer to their Write a Narrative Scene Chart in their writing folders.)

After students have added all of their details, they will need to meet with a peer editor again. This will them help clarify what they have written. When this round of editing is completed, the students are ready to write their scene. Now the prewriting stage is done and it's time to write with sentences at last. You will find that all of this planning will help your students write their scene with vivid details.

Name_____ Date_____

Simple Proofreading Marks Chart

Mark	Meaning
∧	Insert a word, letter, or phrase
ℓ	Delete
≡	Capitalize
/	Change to lowercase
∧⋅	Insert period
⋁	Insert comma
⋁	Insert an apostrophe
⋁ʺ	Insert quotations
#	Insert space
⌒	Close up space
∽	Switch letters or words
¶	Start a new paragraph
(SP)	Check spelling
⌐	Move right
¬	Move left

Write an Action-Reaction Poem

So far, your students have explored the worlds of information and story. Now it is time to live in the moment with the world of poetry. A poem can capture an intense emotional experience. In a poem, the senses are heightened and every word counts. Generalities don't work; it is specific details that make a poem come alive.

Name_____ Date_____

Write an Action-Reaction Poem Chart

1. Make a mind map.

2. Answer the 6 Ws.

3. Think action-reaction.

4. Add details.

5. Write your poem.

Sports are all about action, so students will be asked to write a short action-reaction poem. The prompt says, "What is happening at this moment in time?" This question asks students to think in depth about what happens during that moment. Details, the lifeblood of poetry, will help students complete this writing exercise.

Poetry has three Rs of its own: rhythm, rhyme, and repetition. Although most young students think poetry has to rhyme, writing in rhyme is actually more difficult than writing a free verse poem. A free verse poem doesn't have a pattern to follow, so students can focus on the event itself instead.

Poetry is spoken music, so draw your students' attention to how the words in the poem sound when they are spoken aloud. Changing a word or two changes the rhythm of the line. Where the line ends (or breaks) also affects the rhythm of a poem.

Encourage students to repeat words and phrases, like songwriters do. Repetition helps a poet emphasize a certain action or emotion. Songwriters often repeat an entire paragraph, or stanza. In a song, this repeated stanza is called the *chorus*. In a poem, it is called a *refrain*. Using a refrain is something that older students may wish to try when they write a longer poem.

One short four line stanza is enough to get everyone started. A four line stanza, called a *quatrain*, often has words that rhyme with each other at the end of the second and fourth lines. This will satisfy the needs of those students who feel that they must rhyme. It also means that students only have to find two words that rhyme.

Ask students to focus first on describing the event they are remembering, and then look for words that rhyme. Some students will let go of the need to rhyme at this point, while others will doggedly insist that they must find a word that rhymes. Several rewrites may be necessary to make a poem rhyme, so I recommend that you have copies of what I call "The Magic Word Book" (also known as the thesaurus). Older students may be able to use a rhyming dictionary. If you don't have copies of these books in the classroom, you may wish to use an online resource. Students can type a word into the box on the screen, and the software will show them several possible answers.

The Write an Action-Reaction Poem Chart is in Appendix One with the Moment GO Charts. Use these black line masters to make a copy for each student's writing folder.

Warm-Up

Let's begin by brainstorming. This will help students think about which aspect of the sport they would like to write about. What is happening at this moment in time? The mind map will help them remember, and make a choice.

Hand out copies of the completed Baseball Moment Mind Map GO Chart. Point out that the name of the sport is written in the center of the chart. The other words on the chart are things a player experiences during a single moment in this sport. Ask students to read the words aloud.

The student who created this chart wrote down what was happening at a certain moment in time during this sport. After thinking about what was happening, the student made a decision. That decision is recorded at the bottom of the chart in the "I want to write about" line.

Now it's time for your students to write. After discussing the completed example, hand out blank Mind Map Moment GO Charts for the students to use. Ask them to write the name of the sport in the center circle and create their own mind map.

When each student has a completed mind map, the next step is to make his or her own decision. What moment in time do they want to write about? Ask students to write their decision at the bottom of their chart.

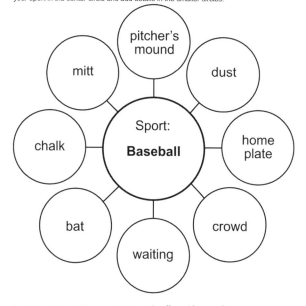

Name Olivia _____ Date January 18 _____

Baseball Moment Mind Map GO Chart

A poem can capture a moment in time. What is happening in this sports moment? Write your sport in the center circle and add details in the smaller circles.

- pitcher's mound
- mitt
- dust
- chalk
- Sport: **Baseball**
- home plate
- bat
- waiting
- crowd

I want to write about this moment in time: __standing at home plate_____

Regulations

Your students have warmed up, so it's time to review the rules. Give each student a copy of the example Baseball 6 Ws GO Chart. Tell your students that these are the six questions that journalists ask (and yes, the last word has a W at the end, not the beginning). Answering the questions the 6 Ws ask will help students focus on the specifics.

Name Olivia   Date January 18

Baseball Moment 6 Ws GO Chart ⚾

Answering the 6 Ws will help you write your sports moment poem.

I want to write about this moment in time: standing at home plate

Who is the main character? me

What happens? I'm standing at home plate

When does it happen? during a game

Where does it happen? at home plate

Why does it happen? my turn to bat

Ho**w** does it happen?

Action: I lift up the bat

Reaction: I stare at the pitcher

Who is the main character?

Will the student be the main character in this poem, or will he or she write about someone else? Who your student chooses as the main character will determine the voice of the poem. Most students write poetry that is also a personal narrative, so they use first person, the "I" voice. Poems about another person are usually written in third person, the "he or she" voice.

What happens?

The simplest answer for this question is what the student writes for the answer to his or her moment in time question.

When does it happen?

Most students will be able to use the answer on the example GO Chart. (This means they already have one-third of the chart filled out.)

Where does it happen?

In the example above, the answer to this question was very similar to another answer. Since we are only focusing on a moment in time, this overlap is fine. (And half of the chart is already completed.)

Why does it happen?

Understanding why a character is at a certain place at a certain time will help us understand that character's motivation.

How does it happen?

You'll notice that this question has two answers. First we want to know what the main character in the poem did. What was that character's action?

To complete the sequence, ask students to write down what happens next. This is the reaction.

In the example above, the main character was responsible for both the action and the reaction. This is a sports poem, so we want to see some sort of movement, even it if it just inside the main character's mind.

After students complete their own GO Chart, ask them to share it with a peer editor. When everyone has "a moment in time," it's time to expand that into a list of specific actions.

The Game

Now that students know what will happen to their poem, they can add details. They already have their actions outlined. An action is followed by reaction. What they need to do now is to turn their list of answers into descriptive phrases. Hand out the example Baseball Moment Poetry Stretch GO Chart for your students to review.

This example page has a poem on it, but the master copies are blank. In this example you will notice that the action and the reaction have been rewritten to form the beginning of the poem. The student added some inner dialogue to give the poem emotion. Encourage your students to add some emotion to their poems.

This poem could also have been written with a focus on the sound of the crowd in the background and the dust blowing as the batter stood at home plate. Those early details were found on the Mind Map Moment GO Chart. Adding those sensory details would result in a completely different poem. It would also give the poem a different emotion.

Each student brings his or her own perspective to their poetry, and that is the beauty of using these GO Charts. Although students begin with the same topic, the resulting poems are always very different.

You'll notice that although I suggested that your students write only four lines, the example poem is longer. Writers in the intermediate grades have often moved beyond simple rhyming poems, so I want to model that. For your lower-level students, writing four lines of poetry is sufficient. (While writing just two or three lines may look easier, it is actually more difficult to describe a moment with so few words.)

As before, I recommend that students share their work with a peer editor. This will help them see if their poem makes sense. The editor will also point out any spelling or grammar errors.

This poem does not have punctuation at the end of each line, a poetic technique called *enjambment*. Punctuation at the end of a line in a poem is called *end stop*.

After students have their poems edited by someone else, they are ready to write the final copy. You can have them use their writing notebooks. Or, as a culminating activity, you can ask each student to type their poem and illustrate it for a class book.

Name Olivia   Date January 18

Baseball Moment Poetry Stretch

Add details to your 6 Ws and stretch your sports moment thoughts into a poem. Write your first draft below.

I lift the bat
and stare
at the pitcher.
Come on!
Throw me
a good one.

Puzzles

The final section of each chapter is a pair of word puzzles. For each sport there is a crossword puzzle and word search puzzle. Working with words is one way to help students learn new vocabulary and reinforce spelling. A crossword puzzle is actually a glossary disguised as a game. The definitions are given as the clues to the puzzle. Word search puzzles have a list of words for students to find in the grid. The answers to the puzzles can be found in Appendix Two.

1

Football

First and Ten Football Readers Theatre Overview

Summary: During a football game, a team tries to move the ball forward 10 yards for a first down.

Readability: 2.1 for entire script (individual levels listed after each part)

Staging: Have the Cougars team players and coach stand together on the left. Place the referee and the two announcers in the middle. The Bears team players and coach can stand together on the right. The students watching on the Cougars' side of the class can be Cougars fans and the students on the Bears' side can be Bears fans.

Props: You may wish to use real football equipment and have the players wear helmets. The referee can blow a real whistle and the two announcers can wear headsets.

Presentation: The players can move their bodies as they act out the game.

Characters

Announcer One: 8 lines (3.6)
Announcer Two: 8 lines (3.3)
Announcer Three: 8 lines (2.7)
Official: 3 lines (3.3)

Cougars Fans: 5 lines (1.6)
Cougars Quarterback: 5 lines (1.4)
Cougars Wide Receiver: 2 lines (2.7)
Cougars Tight End: 2 lines (0.7)
Cougars Running Back: 1 line (0.5)

Bears Fans: 4 lines (1.6)
Bears Defensive Tackle: 4 lines (0.7)
Bears Cornerback: 1 line (1.3)
Bears Linebacker: 1 line (2.6)

First and Ten Football Readers Theatre Script

Announcer One:	Welcome to Thursday afternoon football.
Announcer Two:	The score is Cougars 0, Bears 0.
Cougars Fans:	Go Cougars!
Bears Fans:	Go Bears!
Announcer Three:	It's first and ten.
Announcer One:	The Cougars center snaps the ball.
Cougars Quarterback:	Got it! Now who's open?
Bears Defensive Tackle:	I have to stop the quarterback!
Cougars Wide Receiver:	I have to get away from these linebackers . . .
Cougars Quarterback:	The wide receiver is open.
Announcer Two:	The Cougars quarterback passes the ball to the wide receiver.
Cougars Wide Receiver:	I've got it!
Bears Cornerback:	You're going down!
Announcer Three:	The Bears cornerback makes the tackle.
Announcer One:	The official blows the whistle.
Official:	Shree!
Announcer Two:	The Cougars have advanced two yards.
Cougars Fans:	Go Cougars!
Bears Fans:	Go Bears!
Announcer Three:	The Cougars huddle up and then go to the line.
Announcer One:	It's second and eight.
Announcer Two:	The Cougars center snaps the ball.
Cougars Quarterback:	Here we go . . .
Bears Defensive Tackle:	Must stop the quarterback!
Cougars Tight End:	I'll go the other way.
Cougars Quarterback:	The tight end is open.
Announcer Three:	The Cougars quarterback passes the ball to the tight end.
Cougars Tight End:	Got it!
Bears Linebacker:	Not so fast!
Announcer One:	The Bears linebacker makes the tackle.
Announcer Two:	The official blows the whistle.
Official:	Shree!
Announcer Three:	The Cougars have advanced six more yards.
Cougars Fans:	Go Cougars!
Bears Fans:	Go Bears!

From *Read and Write Sports: Readers Theatre and Writing Activities for Grades 3–8*
by Anastasia Suen. Santa Barbara, CA: Libraries Unlimited. Copyright © 2011.

Announcer One:	The Cougars huddle up and go back to the line.
Announcer Two:	It's third and two.
Announcer Three:	The Cougars center snaps the ball.
Bears Defensive Tackle:	Here I come!
Cougars Quarterback:	Let's try something new.
Announcer One:	The Cougars quarterback hands the ball to the running back.
Cougars Running Back:	I'll go the other way.
Bears Defensive Tackle:	I see you!
Announcer Two:	The Bears defensive tackle brings down the running back.
Announcer Three:	The official blows the whistle.
Official:	Shree! First down!
Announcer One:	It's a first down!
Cougars Fans:	Yay! All right! Woohoo!
Announcer Two:	The Cougars have advanced three yards.
Announcer Three:	We may see some points on the scoreboard soon.
Cougars Fans:	Go Cougars!
Bears Fans:	Go Bears!

Name **Emily**   Date **September 14**

Football Topic Mind Map GO Chart

Write the name of your sport in the center circle and add details in the smaller circles. This brainstorming will help you figure out a research question. What do you want to know about this sport?

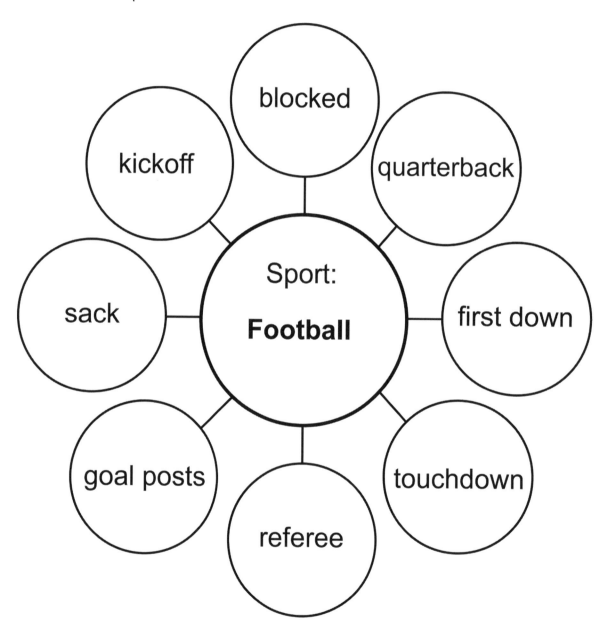

I want to know: **Why isn't a football round?**

From *Read and Write Sports: Readers Theatre and Writing Activities for Grades 3–8* by Anastasia Suen. Santa Barbara, CA: Libraries Unlimited. Copyright © 2011.

Name <u>Emily</u>   Date <u>September 14</u>

Football
Topic
ISP
GO Chart

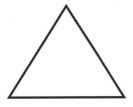

Find the answer to your sports research question with this ISP chart. Use short phrases to record your Information, Source, and Page.

I want to know: <u>Why isn't a football round?</u>

I: <u>U.S. football comes from rugby (in Canada)</u>
S: <u>World Book</u>
P: <u>http://www.worldbookonline.com/</u>

I: <u>rugby comes from soccer (in England)</u>
S: <u>World Book</u>
P: <u>http://www.worldbookonline.com/</u>

I: <u>a football is oval</u>
S: <u>World Book</u>
P: <u>http://www.worldbookonline.com/</u>

I: <u>first rugby balls made from pig's bladder</u>
S: <u>Rugby Football History</u>
P: <u>http://www.rugbyfootballhistory.com/ball.htm</u>

I: <u>football also called a "pigskin"</u>
S: <u>Merriam-Webster</u>
P: <u>http://www.merriam-webster.com/dictionary/pigskin</u>

From *Read and Write Sports: Readers Theatre and Writing Activities for Grades 3–8* by Anastasia Suen. Santa Barbara, CA: Libraries Unlimited. Copyright © 2011.

Football Topic Sandwich GO Chart

Organize the information from your ISP chart so you can write your sports paragraph.

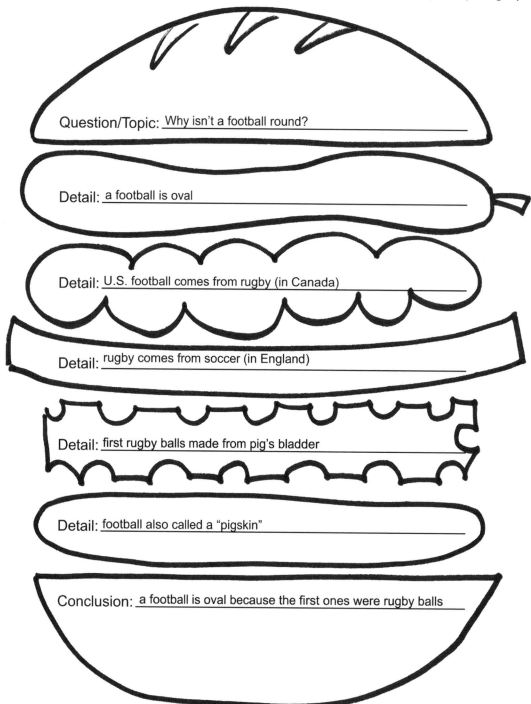

Question/Topic: Why isn't a football round?

Detail: a football is oval

Detail: U.S. football comes from rugby (in Canada)

Detail: rugby comes from soccer (in England)

Detail: first rugby balls made from pig's bladder

Detail: football also called a "pigskin"

Conclusion: a football is oval because the first ones were rugby balls

From *Read and Write Sports: Readers Theatre and Writing Activities for Grades 3–8* by Anastasia Suen. Santa Barbara, CA: Libraries Unlimited. Copyright © 2011.

Name <u>Jacob</u>   Date <u>September 19</u>

Football Scene Mind Map GO Chart

A scene is a small part of a longer story. It is over in a matter of minutes. What can happen in just a few minutes when you play this sport? Write the sport in the center circle and add details in the smaller circles. This will help you decide what aspect of this sport you can write about today.

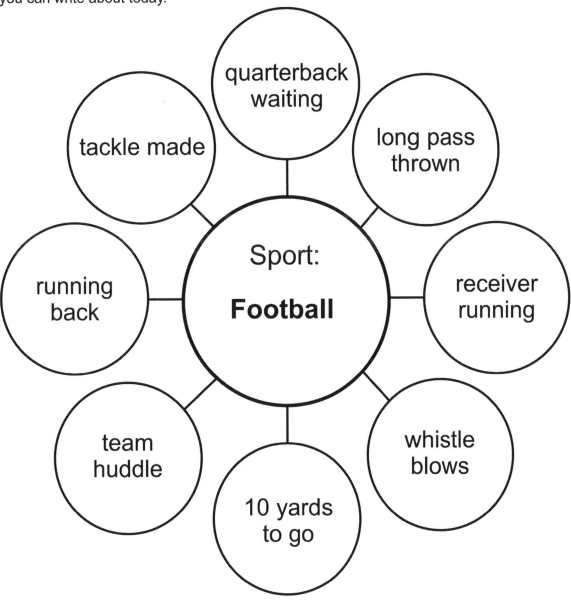

I want to write about: <u>making a first down</u>

Name <u>Jacob</u>   Date <u>September 19</u>

Football Scene Threes GO Chart

Real life goes on and on but a story starts when something changes. Your readers want to find out how someone solves a problem. Where is that person and what is the problem? Decide on the 3 essential elements of your scene. Use short phrases to record your decisions.

I want to write about: <u>making a first down</u>

To write a scene, you need 3 things:

a PERSON: <u>a quarterback</u>

in a PLACE: <u>on a football field during a game</u>

with a PROBLEM: <u>who needs a first down</u>

Name <u>Jacob</u>   Date <u>September 19</u>

Football Scene Story Boxes (Step 1) GO Chart

Step 1: What happens during your scene? Write a short action phrase in each box.

first pass

only moved 2 yards

second pass

6 more yards

third pass

3 more yards

first down!

From *Read and Write Sports: Readers Theatre and Writing Activities for Grades 3–8* by Anastasia Suen. Santa Barbara, CA: Libraries Unlimited. Copyright © 2011.

Name Jacob   Date September 19

Football Scene Story Boxes (Step 2) GO Chart

Step 1: What happens during your scene? Write a short action phrase in each box.

center throws ball	**first pass**	look at field
I catch it		throw to wide receiver
receiver tackled	**only moved 2 yards**	whistle blows
ball down		back to formation
center throws ball	**second pass**	look around
I catch it		throw to tight end
receiver tackled	**6 more yards**	whistle blows
ball down		back to formation
center throws ball	**third pass**	hand off to running back
I catch it		getting excited
back tackled	**3 more yards**	official checks yardage
ball down		anxious
official calls it	**first down!**	back pats
we keep the ball		proud

Step 2: Add 4 details (actions, descriptions, feelings) to each box.

From *Read and Write Sports: Readers Theatre and Writing Activities for Grades 3–8* by Anastasia Suen. Santa Barbara, CA: Libraries Unlimited. Copyright © 2011.

Name Hannah   Date September 27

Football Moment Mind Map GO Chart

A poem can capture a moment in time. What is happening in this sports moment? Write your sport in the center circle and add details in the smaller circles.

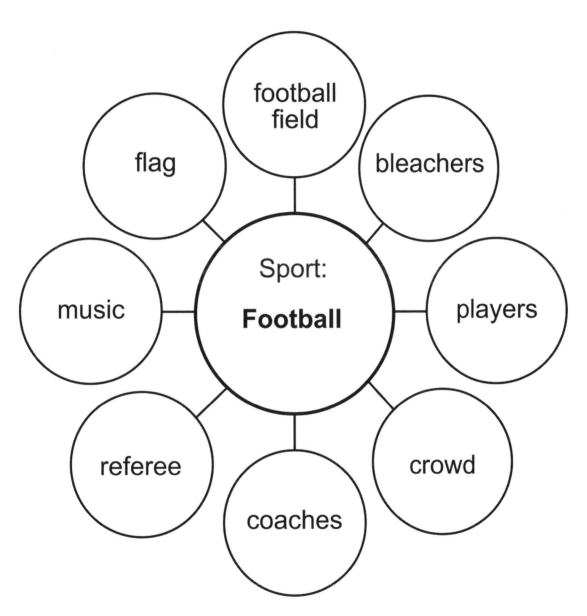

I want to write about this moment in time: making the kickoff

Name <u>Hannah</u>   Date <u>September 27</u>

Football Moment 6 Ws GO Chart

Answering the 6 Ws will help you write your sports moment poem.

I want to write about this moment in time: <u>making the kickoff</u>

Who is the main character? <u>me</u>

What happens? <u>make the kickoff</u>

When does it happen? <u>the beginning of the football game</u>

Where does it happen? <u>on the football field</u>

Why does it happen? <u>it's time to start the game</u>

Ho**w** does it happen?

    Action: <u>I run up to the football on the tee</u>

    Reaction: <u>I kick the ball</u>

From *Read and Write Sports: Readers Theatre and Writing Activities for Grades 3–8* by Anastasia Suen. Santa Barbara, CA: Libraries Unlimited. Copyright © 2011.

Name <u>Hannah</u> Date <u>September 27</u>

Football Moment Poetry Stretch

Add details to your 6 Ws and stretch your sports moment thoughts into a poem. Write your first draft below.

the song is over

the crowd is waiting

it's time for the game to begin

I place the football

on the tee

and walk back a few steps

the whistle blows

the game can begin

I run up to the tee

one

two

three

KICK!

Football Word Search

```
N B V D V A L E L B M U F E N
E M I T F L A H E E R E F E R
K I T C B W L R E V I E C E R
L Y P Y A P C A M S D R A Y U
I T I R R I K W B E F S H Q F
N N F A E G C X K T H Y Q K S
E U G D T S A T E E O L E C I
B P R N N K B O E L Z O S I B
A V I O E I R U B P K F F K T
C K D C C N E C L M H C O C H
K J I E Q W T H D O E W A O U
E Q R S C U R D Z C L S I T D
R N O O W M A O F N M O O N D
L S N R K D U W O I E C B D L
D B L O C K Q N Y P T C J V E
```

block   halftime   linebacker   referee
center   helmet   pigskin   secondary
football   huddle   punt   tackle
fumble   incomplete   quarterback   touchdown
gridiron   kick   receiver   yard

From *Read and Write Sports: Readers Theatre and Writing Activities for Grades 3–8* by Anastasia Suen. Santa Barbara, CA: Libraries Unlimited. Copyright © 2011.

Name_____ Date _____

Football Crossword Puzzle

ACROSS
6 The area at either end of the playing field.
7 A first year player.
8 A free kick to start the game.
10 Another name for the football field.

DOWN
1 The bars on the helmet that cover the player's face.
2 The players on the field come together to talk.
3 To stop a player's movements.
4 A play, from when the ball is in motion until it is ruled dead.
5 A slang name for the football.
9 To run with the football.

2

Basketball

One Point Basketball Readers Theatre Overview

Summary: With the score tied and just 10 seconds left, a player is fouled out—can he make the winning basket?

Readability: 2.6 for entire script (individual levels listed after each part)

Staging: Have the Hawks players and coach stand together on the left. Place the referee and the announcer in the middle. The Wildcats players and coach can stand together on the right. The students watching on the Hawks' side of the class can be Hawks fans and the students on the Wildcats' side can be Wildcats fans.

Props: You may wish to have the students dress out with basketball jerseys for the players and a striped black and white long-sleeved shirt and whistle for the referee.

Presentation: The players can move their bodies as they act out the game.

Characters

> **Announcer**: 13 lines (2.5)
> **Referee**: 4 lines (0.5)
>
> **Hawks Center**: 8 lines (2.1)
> **Hawks Coach**: 3 lines (0.2)
> **Hawks Forward**: 2 lines (0.7)
> **Hawks Guard**: 3 lines (1.2)
> **Hawks Fans**: 7 lines (3.0)
>
> **Wildcats Guard**: 6 lines (1.8)
> **Wildcats Coach**: 2 lines (2.8)
> **Wildcats Center**: 3 lines (1.3)
> **Wildcats Forward**: 2 lines (0.7)
> **Wildcats Fans**: 7 lines (2.9)

One Point Basketball Readers Theatre Script

Announcer:	Just 10 seconds left in the game between the Hawks and the Wildcats and the score is tied.
Hawk Center:	We have to win this game.
Hawks Fans:	Go Hawks!
Wildcats Fans:	Go Wildcats!
Hawks Coach:	Wake up out there!
Hawks Forward:	I can't make the basket from here.
Hawks Center:	I'm open!
Announcer:	The Hawks forward passes the ball to the Hawks center.
Wildcats Coach:	Watch the ball!
Wildcats Guard:	I'm on it.
Hawks Fans:	Go Hawks!
Wildcats Fans:	Go Wildcats!
Announcer:	The Wildcats guard is between the Hawks forward and the basket.
Hawks Center:	Out of my way!
Wildcats Guard:	You wish!
Announcer:	The Hawks center and the Wildcats guard have collided! Both players have hit the hardwood.
Referee:	Shree!
Announcer:	The referee has blown the whistle and stopped the game.
Hawks Center:	Get off me!
Wildcats Guard:	I didn't touch you.
Hawks Center:	Yeah, right . . .
Announcer:	Will they get into a fight with just 3 seconds left? That's no way to win the game.
Hawks Coach:	Don't do it!
Wildcats Coach:	Not now!
Referee:	Come on, break it up.
Wildcats Center:	Let me help you stand up.
Wildcats Guard:	I don't need any help.
Hawks Guard:	Are you all right down there?
Hawks Center:	I'll be fine.
Announcer:	Both players are standing up now waiting for the ref's decision.
Referee:	Personal foul.

Announcer:	The referee is handing the ball to the Hawks center. Will it be a game breaker? If the center makes this basket, the Hawks can win this game.
Hawks Fans:	Make the shot!
Wildcats Fans:	Miss the shot!
Wildcats Forward:	You're not going to make that shot.
Wildcats Guard:	You know it's too hard for you . . .
Wildcats Center:	You'll never make it.
Hawks Guard:	Don't listen to them.
Referee:	Settle down now.
Hawks Fans:	Go Hawks!
Wildcats Fans:	Go Wildcats!
Announcer:	The Hawks center is standing at the free-throw line.
Hawks Fans:	Go Hawks!
Wildcats Fans:	Go Wildcats!
Announcer:	The fans are going wild!
Hawks Fans:	Make the shot!
Wildcats Fans:	Miss the shot!
Hawks Coach:	Focus on the basket . . .
Announcer:	The Hawks center bounces the ball once and stares at the basket. The game is riding on this shot.
Hawks Fans:	Go Hawks!
Wildcats Fans:	Go Wildcats!
Hawks Center:	Here I go . . .
Announcer:	The Hawks center has shot the ball. Will it go in the basket?
Wildcats Guard:	Miss . . .
Hawks Forward:	Go in!
Wildcats Forward:	Miss . . .
Hawks Guard:	Go in!
Wildcats Center:	Miss . . .
Announcer:	The ball goes in the basket. The Hawks are ahead by one point.
Hawks Center:	Yes!

Name **Michael**   Date **October 5**

Basketball Topic Mind Map GO Chart

Write the name of your sport in the center circle and add details in the smaller circles. This brainstorming will help you figure out a research question. What do you want to know about this sport?

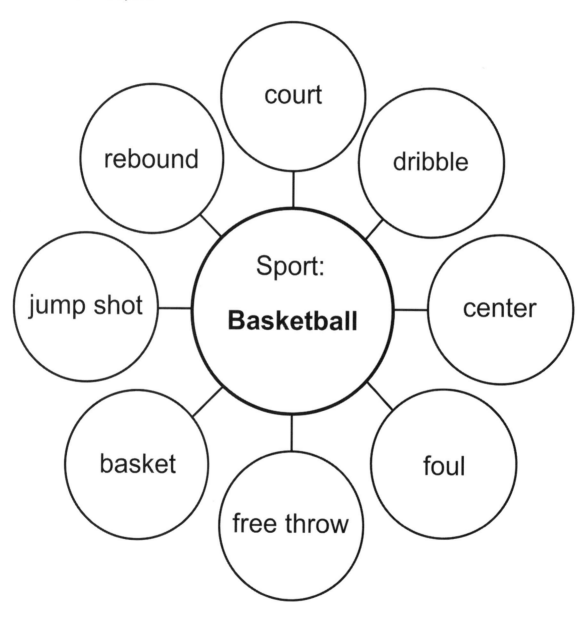

I want to know: **Why is it called a basket?**

Name **Michael**   Date **October 5**

Basketball
Topic
ISP
GO Chart

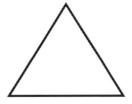

Find the answer to your sports research question with this ISP chart. Use short phrases to record your Information, Source, and Page.

I want to know: **Why is it called a basket?**

I: PE teacher wanted to use boxes for goals, but had none

S: World Book

P: http://www.worldbookonline.com/

I: used peach baskets instead - 1891

S: World Book

P: http://www.worldbookonline.com/

I: 1893 - used hoops with nets

S: Facts on File

P: http://www.fofweb.com/

I: 1913 - used bottomless nets

S: World Book

P: http://www.worldbookonline.com/

I: goals were wooden peach baskets on walls

S: World Almanac for Kids

P: http://www.worldalmanacforkids.com/

Name **Michael**   Date **October 5**

Basketball Topic Sandwich GO Chart

Organize the information from your ISP chart so you can write your sports paragraph.

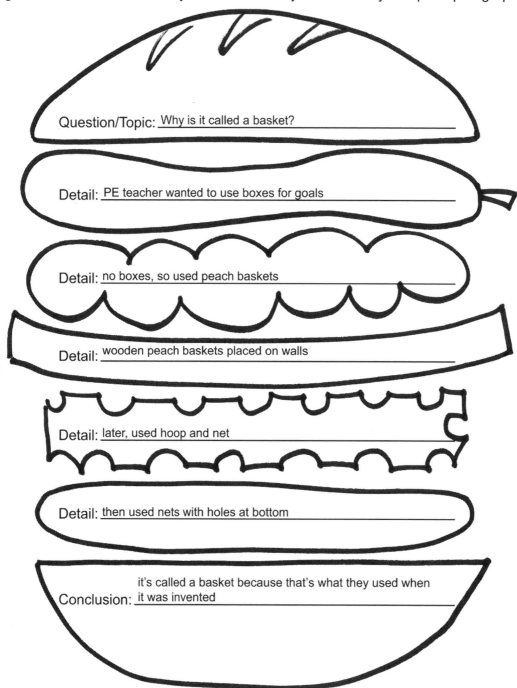

Question/Topic: Why is it called a basket?

Detail: PE teacher wanted to use boxes for goals

Detail: no boxes, so used peach baskets

Detail: wooden peach baskets placed on walls

Detail: later, used hoop and net

Detail: then used nets with holes at bottom

Conclusion: it's called a basket because that's what they used when it was invented

Name <u>Emma</u>   Date <u>October 17</u>

Basketball Scene Mind Map
GO Chart

A scene is a small part of a longer story. It is over in a matter of minutes. What can happen in just a few minutes when you play this sport? Write the sport in the center circle and add details in the smaller circles. This will help you decide what aspect of this sport you can write about today.

I want to write about: <u>making a free throw</u>

Basketball Scene Threes GO Chart

Real life goes on and on but a story starts when something changes. Your readers want to find out how someone solves a problem. Where is that person and what is the problem? Decide on the 3 essential elements of your scene. Use short phrases to record your decisions.

I want to write about: making a free throw

To write a scene, you need 3 things:

a **PERSON:** number 9 on the Hawks team

in a **PLACE:** at the free throw line in a basketball game

with a **PROBLEM:** wants to make a basket

Basketball Scene Story Boxes (Step 1) GO Chart

Step 1: What happens during your scene? Write a short action phrase in each box.

trying to shoot a basket

player knocks me down

ref blows whistle

stand up

walk to free throw line

look at basket

bend knees

shoot ball

From *Read and Write Sports: Readers Theatre and Writing Activities for Grades 3–8* by Anastasia Suen. Santa Barbara, CA: Libraries Unlimited. Copyright © 2011.

Name Emma   Date October 17

Basketball Scene Story Boxes (Step 2) GO Chart

Step 1: What happens during your scene? Write a short action phrase in each box.

number 7 passes the ball	trying to shoot a basket	turn toward basket
I catch it		excited

raise arms to shoot ball	player knocks me down	hit court hard
Wildcats player gets too close		it hurts

calls a foul	ref blows whistle	Wildcats players argue
Wildcats player gets off me		coaches start yelling

number 7 helps me up	stand up	Wildcats glare at me
feel stiff		ref hands me the ball

other players line up	walk to free throw line	turn to face the basket
Wildcats players glare		nervous

breathe deep	look at basket	think success
ignore crowd		focused

bounce ball	bend knees	stare at basket
pull ball in		lift up ball

left go of ball	shoot ball	ball goes in
watch it fly toward net		crowd cheers!

Step 2: Add 4 details (actions, descriptions, feelings) to each box.

From *Read and Write Sports: Readers Theatre and Writing Activities for Grades 3–8* by Anastasia Suen. Santa Barbara, CA: Libraries Unlimited. Copyright © 2011.

Name Joshua   Date October 22

Basketball Moment Mind Map
GO Chart

A poem can capture a moment in time. What is happening in this sports moment? Write
your sport in the center circle and add details in the smaller circles.

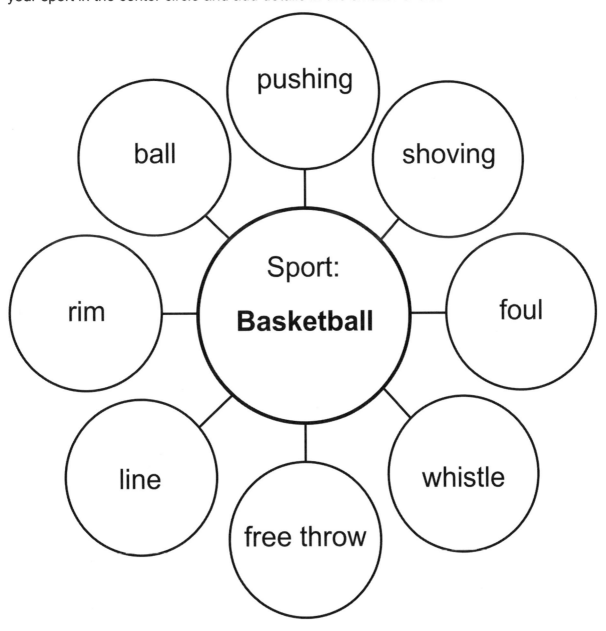

I want to write about this moment in time: shooting a free throw

From *Read and Write Sports: Readers Theatre and Writing Activities for Grades 3–8*
by Anastasia Suen. Santa Barbara, CA: Libraries Unlimited. Copyright © 2011.

Basketball Moment 6 Ws GO Chart

Answering the 6 W's will help you write your sports moment poem.

I want to write about this moment in time: shooting a free throw

Who is the main character? me

What happens? shooting a free throw

When does it happen? during a game

Where does it happen? free throw line

Why does it happen? I was fouled out

How**w** does it happen?

   Action: I stand at the free throw line

   Reaction: I shoot the ball

From Read and Write Sports: Readers Theatre and Writing Activities for Grades 3–8 by Anastasia Suen. Santa Barbara, CA: Libraries Unlimited. Copyright © 2011.

Name **Joshua**   Date **October 22**

Basketball Moment Poetry Stretch

Add details to your 6 Ws and stretch your sports moment thoughts into a poem. Write your first draft below.

They stand beside me

a line on each side

watching me

waiting

beyond us

the crowd is restless

my heart is beating fast

I can do this

I can do this

I bend my knees

and throw the ball...

From *Read and Write Sports: Readers Theatre and Writing Activities for Grades 3–8*
by Anastasia Suen. Santa Barbara, CA: Libraries Unlimited. Copyright © 2011.

Basketball Word Search

```
I Q U R D R G O M K C O L B R
D X W E X R W N N B P O I N T
R G R V D Q A B I A N K F U G
E T R O V A F W U D W O A P N
B R U N G E H T R Z X O S J I
O U Q R J R B U E O Z H T O L
U O L U O F D O L H F E B Y E
N C N T G H S E B B O I R G V
D F U E T B A M B H S I E P A
Z L Q E E S P I I Q Y H A M R
O A L K M R I T R X R L K U T
N H U X I P C S D B R I R J J
E D Y P G G I S S G A J R H R
E K N U D M A L S A C L J M A
L L I N E Z L G P F X T L G E
```

air ball	fast break	line	traveling
assist	forward	point	turnover
block	foul	rebound	zone
buzzer	half court	screen	
carry	hook	slam dunk	
dribble	jump	time out	

From *Read and Write Sports: Readers Theatre and Writing Activities for Grades 3–8* by Anastasia Suen. Santa Barbara, CA: Libraries Unlimited. Copyright © 2011.

Name_____ Date _____

Basketball Crossword Puzzle

ACROSS

1 Getting possession of the basketball after a missed shot.

4 Bouncing the ball on the floor while moving on the court.

5 A shot taken from the middle line of the basketball court.

9 A shot taken while jumping backwards.

10 A blocked shot.

DOWN

2 A player who doesn't pass the ball to his team mates.

3 A shot that misses both the basket and the backboard.

6 An unopposed throw awarded to a player after a foul.

7 A player takes too many steps without dribbling the ball.

8 A player pushes the ball down into the basket with one or both hands.

From *Read and Write Sports: Readers Theatre and Writing Activities for Grades 3–8*
by Anastasia Suen. Santa Barbara, CA: Libraries Unlimited. Copyright © 2011.

3

Hockey

First Goal Hockey Readers Theatre Overview

Summary: A hockey game begins and two teams play until one team scores a goal.

Readability: 1.6 for entire script (individual levels listed after each part)

Staging: Have the Stars team players and coach stand together on the left. Place the referee and the announcer in the middle. The Falcons team players and coach can stand together on the right. The students watching on the Stars' side of the class can be Stars fans and the students on the Falcons' side can be Falcons fans.

Props: You may wish to use real hockey equipment: masks for the players or just the two goalies and a striped black and white long-sleeved shirt for the referee.

Presentation: The players can move their bodies as they act out the game.

Characters

    Announcer: 16 lines (1.0)
    Referee: 2 lines (0.6)

    Stars Fans: 8 lines (0.0)
    Stars Coach: 3 lines (2.0)
    Stars Center: 10 lines (1.7)
    Stars Left Wing: 6 lines (1.3)
    Stars Right Wing: 5 lines (1.3)
    Stars Goalie: 4 lines (0.7)

    Falcons Fans: 7 lines (2.9)
    Falcons Coach: 3 lines (0.0)
    Falcons Defense 1: 3 lines (1.3)
    Falcons Defense 2: 3 lines (1.2)
    Falcons Center: 2 lines (0.4)
    Falcons Right Wing: 4 lines (0.7)
    Falcons Left Wing: 2 lines (0.7)
    Falcons Goalie: 5 lines (1.9)

First Goal Hockey Readers Theatre Script

Announcer:	Today the Stars are playing the Falcons.
Stars Fans:	Go Stars!
Falcons Fans:	Go Falcons!
Stars Coach:	Time to go out on the ice.
Stars Center:	After the face-off, I'll pass it to you.
Stars Left Wing:	I'll be ready.
Falcons Coach:	Stay on their center.
Falcons Defense 1:	Got it, Coach.
Falcons Defense 2:	We will.
Announcer:	Both teams are on the ice. It's time for the game.
Referee:	Are you ready?
Stars Team:	We're ready.
Falcons Team:	We're ready.
Referee:	Here we go . . .
Announcer:	The ref drops the puck.
Stars Center:	I got it . . .
Falcons Center:	Not for long.
Stars Fans:	Go Stars!
Announcer:	The Stars have the puck.
Falcons Coach:	Go after him!
Falcons Right Wing:	We are, we are!
Stars Left Wing:	Pass it . . .
Stars Center:	Here you go.
Announcer:	The Stars Center passes the puck to the Stars Left Wing.
Stars Right Wing:	I'm open.
Stars Fans:	Go Stars!
Announcer:	The puck moves from Left Wing to Right Wing.
Falcons Defense 2:	Not so fast.
Falcons Fans:	Go Falcons!
Stars Right Wing:	I'm blocked! You try it.
Announcer:	The puck goes back to the Stars Center. And now it's flying toward the goal.
Falcons Goalie:	Here it comes.
Stars Fans:	Go Stars!
Stars Right Wing:	Go in the net.
Stars Left Wing:	Go in the net.

Stars Center:	Go in the net.
Falcons Goalie:	Not this time!
Announcer:	. . . and it's blocked! The puck bounces off the goalie's pads.
Falcons Fans:	Go Falcons!
Falcons Coach:	Great play!
Falcons Goalie:	Thanks, Coach.
Announcer:	The Falcons' defense has the puck and is headed towards the other side of the rink.
Falcons Fans:	Go Falcons!
Stars Coach:	Wake up out there.
Stars Left Wing:	I'm on it.
Stars Center:	Here I come.
Stars Fans:	Go Stars!
Falcons Right Wing:	Pass it to me.
Falcons Defense 1:	It's all yours.
Announcer:	The Falcons are moving closer to the goal.
Falcons Fans:	Go Falcons!
Stars Coach:	Watch the crease.
Stars Goalie:	Here they come!
Falcons Right Wing:	Into the goal you go.
Falcons Fans:	Go Falcons!
Announcer:	The puck is moving toward the Stars' goal.
Stars Goalie:	Not so fast.
Announcer:	The Stars' goalie catches the puck with his glove and throws it back on the ice.
Stars Fans:	Go Stars!
Stars Goalie:	Bring it back to the other side, Stars.
Stars Center:	That's the plan.
Announcer:	Now the Stars team is taking the puck to the Falcons' goal.
Falcons Left Wing:	You think you're so good.
Stars Center:	Just watch me.
Announcer:	It's a slap shot. The puck is flying toward the goal. Will it make it?
Stars Fans:	Go Stars!
Stars Right Wing:	Go in the net!
Stars Left Wing:	Go in the net!
Stars Center:	Go in the net!

Announcer: The goalie is reaching for the puck . . .

Falcons Fans: Go Falcons!

Falcons Goalie: No!

Stars Center: Yes!

Announcer: GOOOAAAL! And the score is Stars 1, Falcons 0.

Stars Fans: Go Stars!

Name **Madison** Date **November 2**

Hockey Topic Mind Map GO Chart

Write the name of your sport in the center circle and add details in the smaller circles. This brainstorming will help you figure out a research question. What do you want to know about this sport?

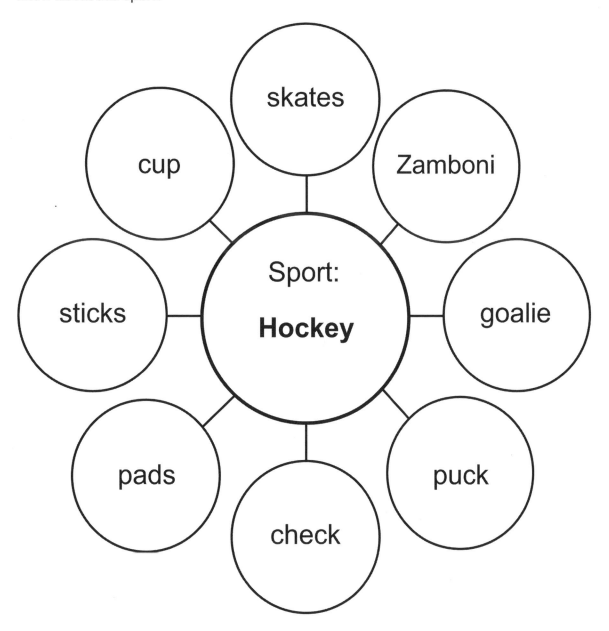

I want to know: <u>Why is the top hockey award called the Stanley Cup?</u>

Name <u>Madison</u> Date <u>November 2</u>

Hockey
Topic
ISP
GO Chart

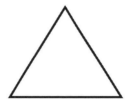

Find the answer to your sports research question with this ISP chart. Use short phrases to record your Information, Source, and Page.

I want to know: <u>Why is the top hockey award called the Stanley Cup?</u>

I: 6th governor of Canada, Lord Stanley of Preston, bought it
S: The Encyclopedia of North American Sports History, Second Edition
P: http://www.fofweb.com/

I: for 1839 hockey championship in Canada
S: The Encyclopedia of North American Sports History, Second Edition
P: http://www.fofweb.com/

I: Stanley donated the silver bowl
S: World Book
P: http://www.worldbookonline.com/

I: silver cup was 7 ½ inches high by 11 ½ inches across
S: NHL
P: http://www.nhl.com/cup/cup.html

I: cost 10 guineas ($50)
S: NHL
P: http://www.nhl.com/cup/cup.html

Name **Madison**   Date **November 2**

Hockey Topic Sandwich GO Chart

Organize the information from your ISP chart so you can write your sports paragraph.

Question/Topic: Why is the top hockey award called the Stanley Cup?

Detail: 6th governor of Canada, Lord Stanley of Preston, bought it

Detail: for 1839 hockey championship in Canada

Detail: silver cup was 7½ inches high by 11½ inches across

Detail: cost 10 guineas ($50)

Detail: Stanley donated the silver bowl

Conclusion: hockey award named after person who started it

From *Read and Write Sports: Readers Theatre and Writing Activities for Grades 3–8*
by Anastasia Suen. Santa Barbara, CA: Libraries Unlimited. Copyright © 2011.

Name Andrew   Date November 13

Hockey Scene Mind Map GO Chart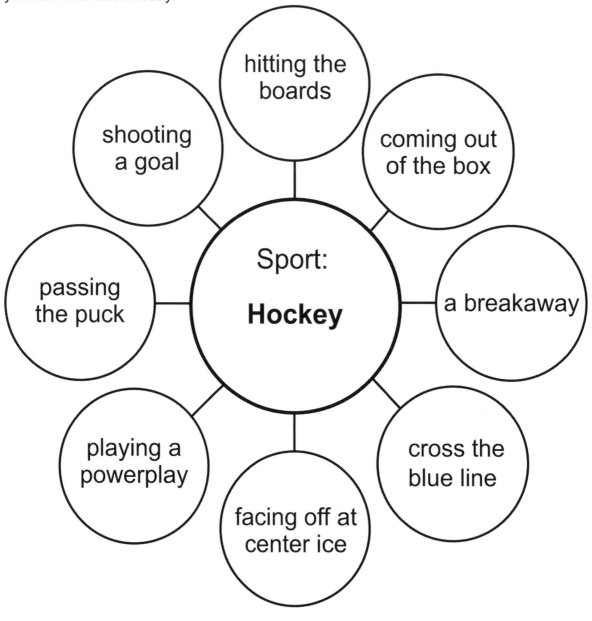

A scene is a small part of a longer story. It is over in a matter of minutes. What can happen in just a few minutes when you play this sport? Write the sport in the center circle and add details in the smaller circles. This will help you decide what aspect of this sport you can write about today.

hitting the boards

shooting a goal

coming out of the box

passing the puck

Sport:

Hockey

a breakaway

playing a powerplay

facing off at center ice

cross the blue line

I want to write about: shooting a goal

From *Read and Write Sports: Readers Theatre and Writing Activities for Grades 3–8* by Anastasia Suen. Santa Barbara, CA: Libraries Unlimited. Copyright © 2011.

Name **Andrew**   Date **November 13**

Hockey Scene Threes GO Chart

Real life goes on and on but a story starts when something changes. Your readers want to find out how someone solves a problem. Where is that person and what is the problem? Decide on the 3 essential elements of your scene. Use short phrases to record your decisions.

I want to write about: **shooting a goal**

To write a scene, you need 3 things:

a **PERSON:** number 5 on the Stars team

in a **PLACE:** on the ice in a hockey game

with a **PROBLEM:** wants to score a goal

Name **Andrew**   Date **November 13**

Hockey Scene Story Boxes (Step 1) GO Chart

Step 1: What happens during your scene? Write a short action phrase in each box.

face-off

team mate passes puck

hit the puck

goal blocked

they shoot for goal

our goalie blocks it

skate to other goal

slapshot

From *Read and Write Sports: Readers Theatre and Writing Activities for Grades 3–8* by Anastasia Suen. Santa Barbara, CA: Libraries Unlimited. Copyright © 2011.

Name **Andrew**   Date **November 13**

Hockey Scene Story Boxes (Step 2) GO Chart

Step 1: What happens during your scene? Write a short action phrase in each box.

stick down	**face-off**	watch Falcons center
watch ref		hit to puck Stars player

catch puck with stick	**team mate passes puck**	others follow
skate toward goal		determined

look at the goal	**hit the puck**	swing
see an opening		crowd cheers

puck hits goalie's pad	**goal blocked**	Falcons get puck
puck bounces onto ice		mad

skate after Falcons	**they shoot for goal**	Falcons shoot puck at goal
coach yells		frustrated

goalie passes puck	**our goalie blocks it**	stop puck with stick
skate after puck		crowd cheering

Stars follow me	**skate to other goal**	cross blue line
cross red line		see an opening

goalie reaches for puck	**slapshot**	crowd cheers
goalie misses		elated!

Step 2: Add 4 details (actions, descriptions, feelings) to each box.

From *Read and Write Sports: Readers Theatre and Writing Activities for Grades 3–8*
by Anastasia Suen. Santa Barbara, CA: Libraries Unlimited. Copyright © 2011.

Name **Sarah**   Date **November 28**

Hockey Moment Mind Map GO Chart

A poem can capture a moment in time. What is happening in this sports moment? Write your sport in the center circle and add details in the smaller circles.

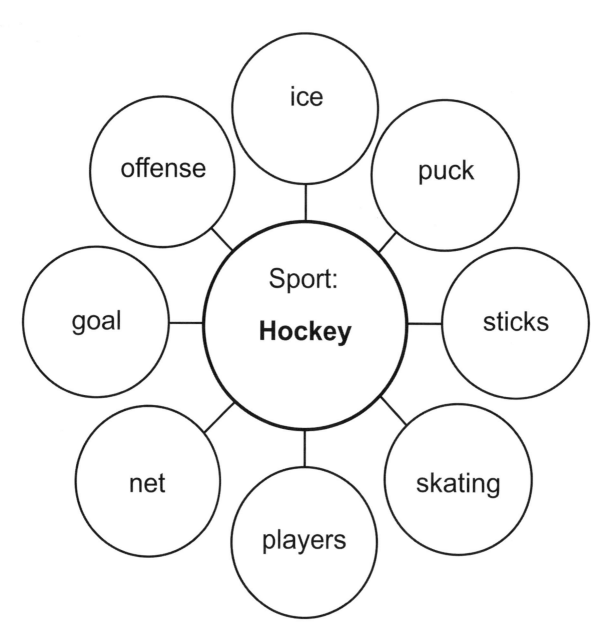

I want to write about this moment in time: **hitting the puck**

Hockey Moment 6 Ws GO Chart

Answering the 6 Ws will help you write your sports moment poem.

I want to write about this moment in time: hitting the puck

Who is the main character? me

What happens? I hit the puck towards the net

When does it happen? during a game

Where does it happen? on the ice

Why does it happen? I see an opening

How does it happen?

    Action: I swing my stick

    Reaction: the puck flies toward the goal

From *Read and Write Sports: Readers Theatre and Writing Activities for Grades 3–8* by Anastasia Suen. Santa Barbara, CA: Libraries Unlimited. Copyright © 2011.

Hockey Moment Poetry Stretch

Add details to your 6 Ws and stretch your sports moment thoughts into a poem. Write your first draft below.

I swing

my stick

HARD.

The puck

FLIES

toward the net.

Go in...

Go in...

Go in...

GOAL!

Hockey Word Search

```
J W Y P H E C C F F O E C A F
R I N K E D E F E N S E M E N
Z O I S L N C R E A S E L P E
N X T L M E A Q C C F E R T I
F O H A E C G L S H E T E G L
C E I P T A C B T N V I B B A
J E O S V G M N O Y N U O P O
G R L H S E Q Z A O C F U V G
N E P O U I L G B M F Z N M S
I F H T T A M M Z S S H D M V
W E A S R E A R I M I E I V Y
U R R T E Z A D E R E T N E C
D H U I L S E M U T C L Z I P
P E Z C P R J N G S N M Q C L
N R K K C U P N L P H I B O N
```

cage	helmet	puck	team
center	intermission	rebound	wing
crease	linesman	referee	Zamboni
defensemen	neutral zone	rink	
face-off	offside	slapshot	
goalie	penalty	stick	

Name_____ Date _____

Hockey Crossword Puzzle

ACROSS

2 The wall around a hockey rink.

3 When the goalie blocks a shot

6 When a player crosses the blue line before the puck.

7 Three goals in one game scored by one player.

8 When one team has more players on the ice than the other team

9 An official drops the puck between the sticks of two opposing players.

DOWN

1 The area in front of the goal.

2 The glove the goalie wears on the hand that holds the stick.

4 The center ice between the two blue lines.

5 The glove the goalie wears on the non-stick hand.

From *Read and Write Sports: Readers Theatre and Writing Activities for Grades 3–8* by Anastasia Suen. Santa Barbara, CA: Libraries Unlimited. Copyright © 2011.

4

Skating

Roller Skating Race Readers Theatre Overview

Summary: There are six Saturday afternoon birthday parties at Sam's Roller Rink and Restaurant and now it's time for the races. Who will win?

Readability: 0.1 for entire script (individual levels listed after each part)

Staging: The skaters can stand in numerical order from left to right, followed by the owner, Sam, and the narrator.

Props: You may wish to have Sam and the skaters wear skates as they read this play.

Presentation: The players can move their bodies as they act out the race.

Characters

> **Narrator**: 9 lines (4.2)
> **Sam**: 8 lines (0.0)
> **Crowd**: 12 lines (3.4)
>
> **Skater One**: 16 lines (0.9)
> **Skater Two**: 8 lines (0.1)
> **Skater Three**: 7 lines (0.2)
> **Skater Four**: 7 lines (1.3)
> **Skater Five**: 5 lines (2.5)
> **Skater Six**: 2 lines (3.4)

Roller Skating Race Readers Theatre Script

Narrator:	It's Saturday afternoon at Sam's Roller Rink and Restaurant. There are six birthday parties going on at once. The music is blasting and the skates are rolling.
Skater One:	There are so many kids here!
Skater Two:	Yeah, isn't it great?
Skater Three:	When are they going to let the big kids race?
Skater Four:	The little kids always race first.
Sam:	Are you ready to race?
Crowd:	Yeah!
Sam:	On your mark, get set, go!
Crowd:	Go! Go! Go!
Skater One:	Look at the little kids go!
Skater Two:	They're falling all over the place!
Skater Three:	This is wild!
Skater Four:	It's always like this when the little kids race.
Crowd:	Go! Go! Go!
Skater One:	Here they come!
Skater Two:	It looks like the kid with the orange hat will win.
Skater Three:	I want the one with the purple jacket to win.
Crowd:	Go! Go! Go!
Skater Four:	Who will cross the finish line first?
Crowd:	Go! Go! Go!
Sam:	And the winner is . . .
Skater One:	The kid with the green shirt came out of nowhere!
Narrator:	Sam lifts the winner's hand into the air.
Crowd:	Yeah!
Sam:	It's time for the next race.
Narrator:	As the little kids skated off the rink, the big kids skated onto the rink. Everyone was talking at once.
Crowd:	Talk. Talk. Talk. Talk. Talk.
Skater One:	Yeah, now it's our turn.
Skater Two:	It's show time!
Skater Three:	I'm going to win this one.
Skater Four:	No, I'm going to win this one.
Sam:	Line up for the next race here.
Skater One:	I want to be near the center of the rink.
Skater Two:	I think the middle is best.

Skater Three:	Stand over here by me.
Skater Four:	The distance is shortest near the center of the rink.
Narrator:	Another skater comes to the line at the middle of the rink with a push.
Skater Five:	Out of my way.
Skater One:	Hey! I was here first.
Skater Five:	This is my spot.
Sam:	Settle down now . . . Are you ready to race?
All Skaters:	Yes!
Sam:	On your mark, get set . . . GO!
Crowd:	Go! Go! Go!
Narrator:	The skaters surge across the starting line.
Skater Five:	Out of my way.
Skater One:	Hey!
Narrator:	Uh-oh, one of the skaters has already fallen.
Skater One:	Ouch!
Narrator:	The skaters are going around the first turn.
Crowd:	Go! Go! Go!
Skater One:	I have to catch up!
Crowd:	Go! Go! Go!
Skater Five:	Out of my way.
Skater Six:	What?
Narrator:	Uh-oh, two skaters have collided.
Skater One:	It's the same kid who tripped me!
Crowd:	Go! Go! Go!
Skater One:	I'm almost at the finish line.
Crowd:	Go! Go! Go!
Skater One:	I made it!
Skater Two:	About time you got here.
Skater One:	That kid tripped me!
Skater Three:	I saw that.
Skater Four:	It didn't work the second time.
Skater One:	Ha! What goes around, comes around.
Sam:	And the winner is . . .
Narrator:	Sam lifts the winner's hand into the air.
Skater Two:	I won on my birthday!
Crowd:	Yeah!

Name **Matthew**   Date **December 6**

Skating Topic Mind Map GO Chart

Write the name of your sport in the center circle and add details in the smaller circles. This brain storming will help you figure out a research question. What do you want to know about this sport?

I want to know: **When were the first skates used?**

From *Read and Write Sports: Readers Theatre and Writing Activities for Grades 3–8* by Anastasia Suen. Santa Barbara, CA: Libraries Unlimited. Copyright © 2011.

Name **Matthew**   Date **December 6**

Skating
Topic
ISP
GO Chart

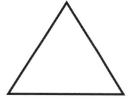

Find the answer to your sports research question with this ISP chart. Use short phrases to record your Information, Source, and Page.

I want to know: **When were the first skates used?**

I: ice skates from 50 BC found in London

S: World Book

P: http://www.worldbookonline.com/

I: skate blades made from polished animal bones and leather

S: World Book

P: http://www.worldbookonline.com/

I: animal bone skates from 3000 BC found in Switzerland

S: Ice Skates webpage

P: http://inventors.about.com/library/inventors/bliceskates.htm

I: old Dutch word for skate is "leg bone"

S: Ice Skates webpage

P: http://inventors.about.com/library/inventors/bliceskates.htm

I: in Scandinavia as early as 1000 BC

S: Encyclopaedia Britannica

P: http://www.britannica.com/EBchecked/topic/281190/ice-skating

Name **Matthew**   Date **December 6**

Skating Topic Sandwich GO Chart

Organize the information from your ISP chart so you can write your sports paragraph.

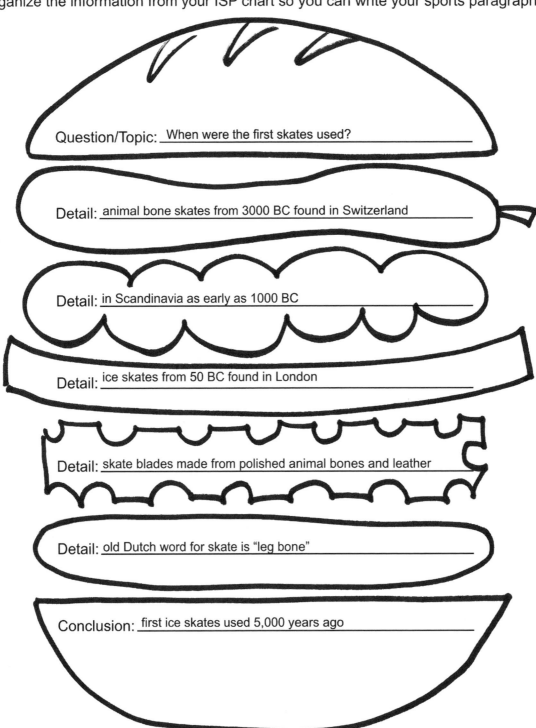

Question/Topic: When were the first skates used?

Detail: animal bone skates from 3000 BC found in Switzerland

Detail: in Scandinavia as early as 1000 BC

Detail: ice skates from 50 BC found in London

Detail: skate blades made from polished animal bones and leather

Detail: old Dutch word for skate is "leg bone"

Conclusion: first ice skates used 5,000 years ago

From *Read and Write Sports: Readers Theatre and Writing Activities for Grades 3–8* by Anastasia Suen. Santa Barbara, CA: Libraries Unlimited. Copyright © 2011.

Name **Alexis**   Date **December 8**

Skating Scene Mind Map GO Chart

A scene is a small part of a longer story. It is over in a matter of minutes. What can happen in just a few minutes when you play this sport? Write the sport in the center circle and add details in the smaller circles. This will help you decide what aspect of this sport you can write about today.

I want to write about: **racing**

From Read and Write Sports: Readers Theatre and Writing Activities for Grades 3–8
by Anastasia Suen. Santa Barbara, CA: Libraries Unlimited. Copyright © 2011.

Skating Scene Threes GO Chart

Real life goes on and on but a story starts when something changes. Your readers want to find out how someone solves a problem. Where is that person and what is the problem? Decide on the 3 essential elements of your scene. Use short phrases to record your decisions.

I want to write about: racing

To write a scene, you need 3 things:

a **PERSON:** a friend

in a **PLACE:** at a birthday party at a skating rink

with a **PROBLEM:** wants to win the race

From *Read and Write Sports: Readers Theatre and Writing Activities for Grades 3–8* by Anastasia Suen. Santa Barbara, CA: Libraries Unlimited. Copyright © 2011.

Skating Scene Story Boxes (Step 1) GO Chart

Step 1: What happens during your scene? Write a short action phrase in each box.

watch the little kids race

hear call for the next race

another kid bumps me

race begins

the other kid trips me

race fast

the other kid trips someone else

cross the finish line

From *Read and Write Sports: Readers Theatre and Writing Activities for Grades 3–8* by Anastasia Suen. Santa Barbara, CA: Libraries Unlimited. Copyright © 2011.

Skating Scene Story Boxes (Step 2) GO Chart

Step 1: What happens during your scene? Write a short action phrase in each box.

at skating rink	**watch the little kids race**	wearing roller skates
with friends from party		impatient

little kids skate off	**hear call for the next race**	party friends skate over
lots of pushing		we line up

pushes to the center spot	**another kid bumps me**	kid won't apologize
almost fall		mad

"On your mark, get set..."	**race begins**	big rush at starting line
whistle blows		excited

I fall	**the other kid trips me**	left behind
hit my knee		I have to catch up

swing arms	**race fast**	go into first turn
lean forward		knee hurts

they both fall	**the other kid trips someone else**	I skate around them
other kid yells		have to hurry

friends cheer	**cross the finish line**	friends pat me on the back
happy I made it		race over!

Step 2: Add 4 details (actions, descriptions, feelings) to each box.

Name **Ethan** _____ Date **December 12** _____

Skating Moment Mind Map GO Chart

A poem can capture a moment in time. What is happening in this sports moment? Write your sport in the center circle and add details in the smaller circles.

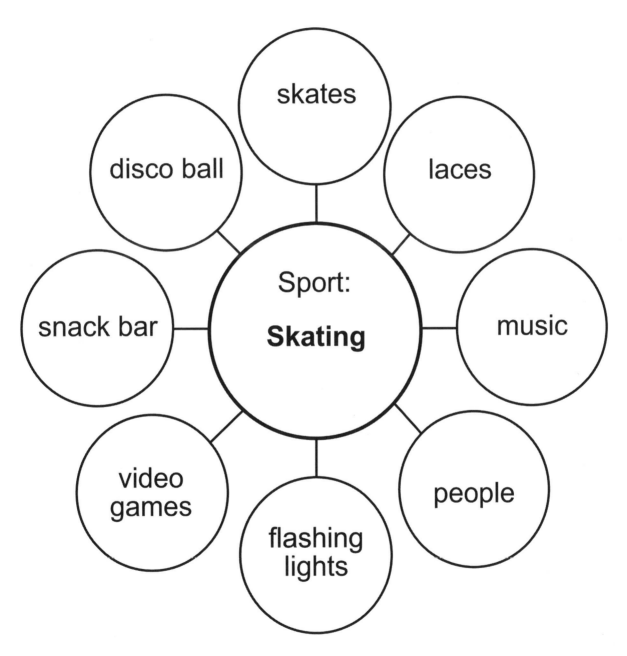

I want to write about this moment in time: **skating to loud music** _____

From *Read and Write Sports: Readers Theatre and Writing Activities for Grades 3–8* by Anastasia Suen. Santa Barbara, CA: Libraries Unlimited. Copyright © 2011.

Name <u>Ethan</u>   Date <u>December 12</u>

Skating Moment 6 Ws GO Chart

Answering the 6 Ws will help you write your sports moment poem.

I want to write about this moment in time: <u>skating to loud music</u>

Who is the main character? <u>me</u>

What happens? <u>skating to loud music</u>

When does it happen? <u>on the weekend</u>

Where does it happen? <u>at the skating rink</u>

Why does it happen? <u>It's free skate time</u>

Ho**w** does it happen?

     Action: <u>the DJ turns up the music</u>

     Reaction: <u>I skate around the rink</u>

Name **Ethan** _____ Date **December 12** _____

Skating Moment Poetry Stretch

Add details to your 6 Ws and stretch your sports moment thoughts into a poem. Write
your first draft below.

ba-bump

ba-bump

the music plays

left leg

right leg

glide

round

and

round

under

flashing

lights

I pump

I skate

I fly!

From _Read and Write Sports: Readers Theatre and Writing Activities for Grades 3–8_
by Anastasia Suen. Santa Barbara, CA: Libraries Unlimited. Copyright © 2011.

Skating Word Search

```
Y P M U J E L P I R T O Z O Y O
B E U Q S E B A R A D C A M E L
O P R O G R A M U E G N U L C T
H R L S C R O S S O V E R S O N
S J T G E V I G F J F U E G M E
H L W S F N O Z C K O V J K P M
M M A O I F I S C S Q U N J U E
C O G N R L E V P T R J D D L L
K K K R O L A R E E P I I K S E
R L Y J G I D D V P T I A A O S
O T O N V C T S E S A S V P R B
W P I L J V Y A P M P R E O Y D
T S B T E A M V N Z D I G O T R
O Z B A C K F L I P D L R X T X
O C X V N E L Z Z I W S O A V W
F G D O U B L E Q T N M I G L X
```

arabesque	element	pairs	toe step
backflip	footwork	pivot	triple jump
camel	gold medalist	program	worlds
compulsory	grapevines	singles	
crossovers	lunge	spiral	
double	nationals	swizzle	

From *Read and Write Sports: Readers Theatre and Writing Activities for Grades 3–8*
by Anastasia Suen. Santa Barbara, CA: Libraries Unlimited. Copyright © 2011.

Name_____ Date_____

Skating Crossword Puzzle

ACROSS
1 Two people skating together.
5 Two or more jumps or spins in a row.
6 A small jump.
8 The wall around the ice rink.
9 Patterns skated in the ice.
10 Sharp part of the skate blade.

DOWN
2 Three or four wheels in a single line.
3 Competition to select the national champion.
4 Flat surface for skating.
7 One skater performing for a judge.

From *Read and Write Sports: Readers Theatre and Writing Activities for Grades 3–8*
by Anastasia Suen. Santa Barbara, CA: Libraries Unlimited. Copyright © 2011.

5

Baseball

Hey, Batter, Batter! Baseball Readers Theatre Overview

Summary: During a baseball game, a batter tries to hit the ball and get on base.

Readability: 3.9 for entire script (individual levels listed after each part)

Staging: From left to right, (behind the plate) the two announcers, (at the plate) the umpire, the Badgers catcher and the Orioles batter, face an empty middle space and then the order continues with the Badgers pitcher and the Badgers outfielder both facing the plate.

Props: You may wish to use real baseball equipment: a bat for the batter, masks for the catcher and umpire, and gloves for the catcher, pitcher, and outfielder. The simplest props would be baseball caps for the umpire and players and two pieces of cardboard for the plate and the pitcher's mound.

Presentation: The players can move their bodies as they act out the game.

Characters

> **Announcer One**: 9 lines (3.2)
> **Announcer Two**: 9 lines (2.4)
> **Umpire**: 2 lines (3.0)
> **Crowd**: 14 lines (3.5)
>
> **Orioles Batter**: 12 lines (1.0)
>
> **Badgers Pitcher**: 3 lines (2.0)
> **Badgers Catcher**: 2 lines (2.2)
> **Badgers Outfielder**: 4 lines (0.7)

Hey, Batter, Batter! Baseball Readers Theatre Script

Announcer One:	Number seven on the Orioles is coming up to bat.
Orioles Batter:	I have to hit this.
Announcer Two:	Number seven lifts the bat.
Crowd:	Hey, batter, batter! Hey, batter, batter! Swing!
Orioles Batter:	Okay, pitcher. Give me something good.
Crowd:	Hey, batter, batter! Hey, batter, batter! Swing!
Announcer One:	The Badgers' pitcher winds up.
Badgers Pitcher:	Here it comes!
Crowd:	Hey, batter, batter! Hey, batter, batter! Swing!
Orioles Batter:	I can hit it!
Announcer Two:	The Orioles' batter swings.
Badgers Catcher:	Right in the glove.
Umpire:	Strike one!
Announcer One:	The Badgers catcher throws the ball back to the pitcher.
Crowd:	Hey, batter, batter! Hey, batter, batter! Swing!
Announcer Two:	And the Badgers' pitcher winds up.
Crowd:	Hey, batter, batter! Hey, batter, batter! Swing!
Badgers Pitcher:	Here it comes!
Crowd:	Hey, batter, batter! Hey, batter, batter! Swing!
Orioles Batter:	I'll hit this one!
Announcer One:	The Orioles' batter swings.
Badgers Catcher:	Right in the glove.
Umpire:	Strike two!
Orioles Batter:	How did I miss that?
Announcer Two:	The catcher stands and throws the ball back to the pitcher.
Badgers Pitcher:	One more strike and this one is out.
Orioles Batter:	One more strike and I'm out!
Announcer One:	Number seven lifts the bat.
Crowd:	Hey, batter, batter! Hey, batter, batter! Swing!
Announcer Two:	The pitcher winds up . . .
Crowd:	Hey, batter, batter! Hey, batter, batter! Swing!
Announcer One:	And throws.
Crowd:	Hey, batter, batter! Hey, batter, batter! Swing!
Orioles Batter:	I'll hit this . . .
Announcer Two:	And the batter swings.
Crowd:	CRACK!

Orioles Batter:	I hit it!
Crowd:	Run!
Announcer One:	The ball is going into left field.
Orioles Batter:	I have to run to first base.
Badgers Outfielder:	The ball is coming my way.
Crowd:	Run!
Announcer Two:	The outfielder is running toward the ball.
Announcer One:	Number seven is running toward first base.
Orioles Batter:	I'm almost there.
Badgers Outfielder:	I'm almost there.
Crowd:	Run!
Orioles Batter:	I made it!
Announcer Two:	The Badgers' outfielder jumps up.
Badgers Outfielder:	I . . .
Announcer One:	The ball has gone over the fence!
Badgers Outfielder:	It's a home run!
Announcer Two:	It's a home run!
Orioles Batter:	It's a home run!
Crowd:	Hooray!

Name Abigail   Date January 9

Baseball Topic Mind Map GO Chart

Write the name of your sport in the center circle and add details in the smaller circles.
This brainstorming will help you figure out a research question. What do you want to
know about this sport?

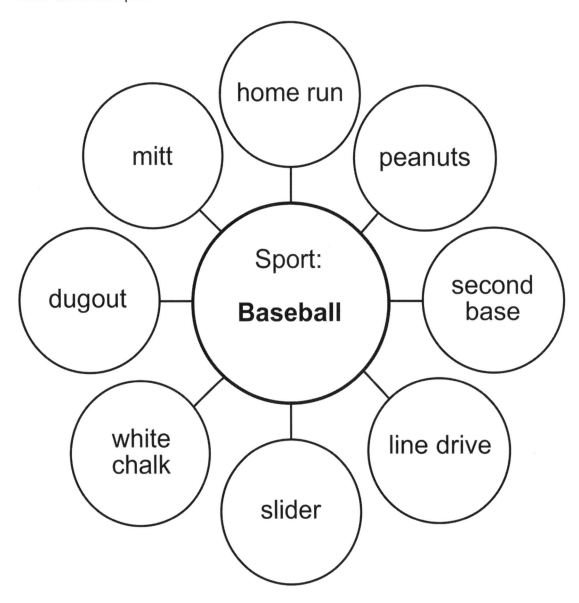

I want to know: Where did baseball come from?

From *Read and Write Sports: Readers Theatre and Writing Activities for Grades 3–8*
by Anastasia Suen. Santa Barbara, CA: Libraries Unlimited. Copyright © 2011.

Baseball
Topic
ISP
GO Chart

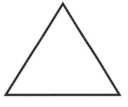

Find the answer to your sports research question with this ISP chart. Use short phrases to record your Information, Source, and Page.

I want to know: Where did baseball come from?

I: think it came from a game called rounders
S: Library of Congress
P: http://www.americaslibrary.gov/cgi-bin/page.cgi/jp/bball/early_1

I: the bases in rounders are poles (1760 book)
S: Library of Congress
P: http://www.americaslibrary.gov/jp/bball/jp_bball_early_1_e.html

I: baseball like rounders but not the same
S: baseball history webpage
P: http://www.solarnavigator.net/sport/baseball.htm

I: rounders has 4 bases and "home"
S: Rounder's League page
P: http://buryrounders.org.uk/thegame.htm

I: to score, you hit the ball with a bat and run around the 4 bases
S: Cornwall sports league
P: http://www.cornwallsportspartnership.co.uk/sports/rounders

Name Abigail   Date January 9

Baseball Topic Sandwich GO Chart

Organize the information from your ISP chart so you can write your sports paragraph.

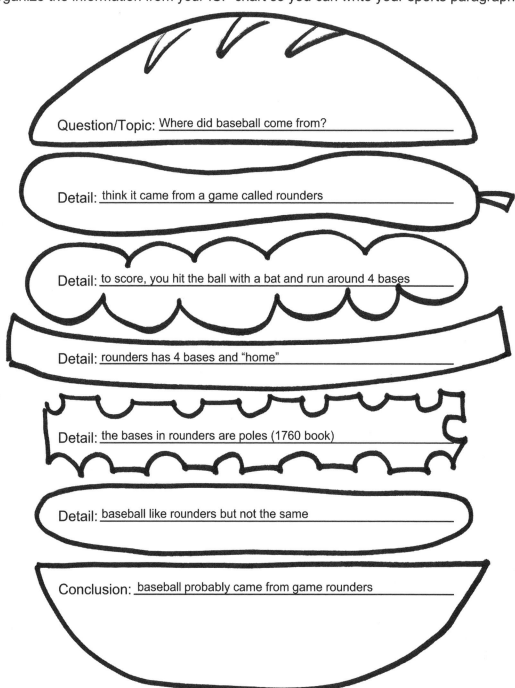

Question/Topic: Where did baseball come from?

Detail: think it came from a game called rounders

Detail: to score, you hit the ball with a bat and run around 4 bases

Detail: rounders has 4 bases and "home"

Detail: the bases in rounders are poles (1760 book)

Detail: baseball like rounders but not the same

Conclusion: baseball probably came from game rounders

Name Joseph   Date January 11

Baseball Scene Mind Map GO Chart

A scene is a small part of a longer story. It is over in a matter of minutes. What can happen in just a few minutes when you play this sport? Write the sport in the center circle and add details in the smaller circles. This will help you decide what aspect of this sport you can write about today.

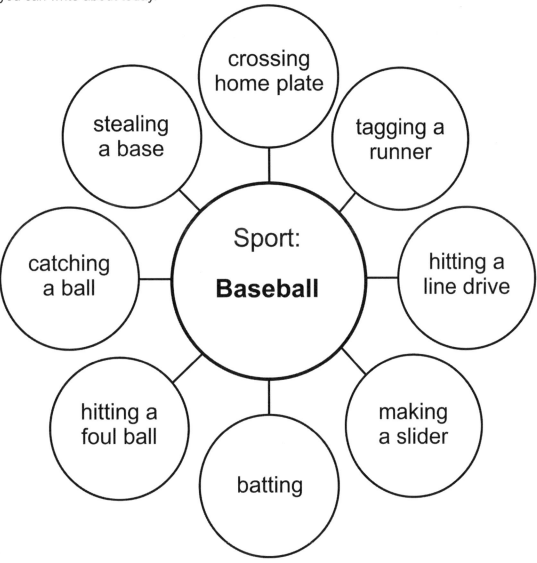

I want to write about: batting _____

Name Joseph   Date January 11

Baseball Scene Threes GO Chart

Real life goes on and on but a story starts when something changes. Your readers want to find out how someone solves a problem. Where is that person and what is the problem? Decide on the 3 essential elements of your scene. Use short phrases to record your decisions.

I want to write about: batting

To write a scene, you need 3 things:

a **PERSON:** number 7 on the Orioles

in a **PLACE:** at a home plate in a baseball game

with a **PROBLEM:** going to bat to try and hit the ball

Name Joseph   Date January 11

Baseball Scene Story Boxes (Step 1) GO Chart

Step 1: What happens during your scene? Write a short action phrase in each box.

walks to home plate

swings the bat

swings the bat

hits the ball

runs to first base

Baseball Scene Story Boxes (Step 2) GO Chart

Step 1: What happens during your scene? Write a short action phrase in each box.

#7 on the Orioles wants to get a hit	**walks to home plate**	raises the bat hoping for a good pitch
looks at the pitcher's shirt Badgers' pitcher winds up	**swings the bat**	the ball comes surprised it was a miss
looks at grass in outfield the pitcher winds up	**swings the bat**	the ball comes upset at second miss
the pitcher winds up loud sound when bat hits	**hits the ball**	crowd yells ball goes to left field
drops bat on ground touches first base	**runs to first base**	makes it in time happy

Step 2: Add 4 details (actions, descriptions, feelings) to each box.

From *Read and Write Sports: Readers Theatre and Writing Activities for Grades 3–8* by Anastasia Suen. Santa Barbara, CA: Libraries Unlimited. Copyright © 2011.

Name Olivia   Date January 18

Baseball Moment Mind Map
GO Chart

A poem can capture a moment in time. What is happening in this sports moment? Write
your sport in the center circle and add details in the smaller circles.

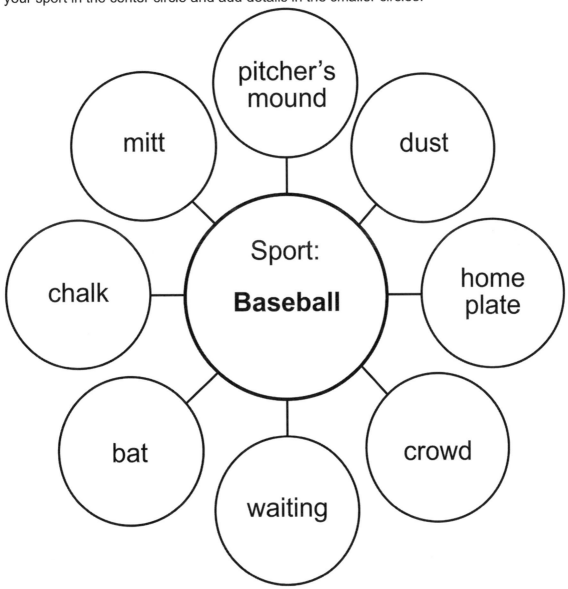

I want to write about this moment in time: standing at home plate

From *Read and Write Sports: Readers Theatre and Writing Activities for Grades 3–8*
by Anastasia Suen. Santa Barbara, CA: Libraries Unlimited. Copyright © 2011.

Name Olivia   Date January 18

Baseball Moment 6 Ws GO Chart

Answering the 6 Ws will help you write your sports moment poem.

I want to write about this moment in time: standing at home plate

Who is the main character? me

What happens? I'm standing at home plate

When does it happen? during a game

Where does it happen? at home plate

Why does it happen? my turn to bat

How does it happen?

     Action: I lift up the bat

     Reaction: I stare at the pitcher

Name Olivia   Date January 18

Baseball Moment Poetry Stretch

Add details to your 6 Ws and stretch your sports moment thoughts into a poem. Write
your first draft below.

I lift the bat

and stare

at the pitcher.

Come on!

Throw me

a good one.

From *Read and Write Sports: Readers Theatre and Writing Activities for Grades 3–8*
by Anastasia Suen. Santa Barbara, CA: Libraries Unlimited. Copyright © 2011.

Baseball Word Search

```
F D C Z T X I T F O A W I L C
B U I X J O E V B X B K I D B
Q T Q A W U Y X A L A M M Y T
Y Q U Z V O E W T O S K T N O
M E H O M E R L T X E T U I U
R C K D O Y R L I Q S F O Z H
T S Y I W A U A N C P I T C H
S T R D R E S B G U L E U E M
R E M E K T L S C E F L H O V
O A K U T T S B I Q W D S F E
R L Z K N W F C U S R I K E F
R Z T U R L T I V O T H J H L
E Q B U F O U L R E D Q P N Y
H S I N G L E U A Z K V V F R
V N X S C F N V E L P I R T L
```

assist	double	homer	steal
average	errors	out	strike
ball	field	pitch	triple
bases	fly	run	
batting	foul	shutout	
bunt	hit	single	

From *Read and Write Sports: Readers Theatre and Writing Activities for Grades 3–8* by Anastasia Suen. Santa Barbara, CA: Libraries Unlimited. Copyright © 2011.

Baseball Crossword Puzzle

ACROSS

2 The place where the game is played.
3 Hitting the ball a very short distance.
4 When a player goes to one extra base.
7 A mistake.
8 A long object used to hit the ball.
10 A ball is hit over the outfield fence.

DOWN

1 What the bat does to the ball.
2 The ball is hit out of bounds.
3 The round object used in this game.
5 A player's score at bat.
6 The player who stands on the mound.
9 Each side has three per inning.

6

Soccer

First Point Soccer Readers Theatre Overview

Summary: A soccer game begins and two teams try to score the first point.

Readability: 0.9 for entire script (individual levels listed after each part)

Staging: Have the Chargers' team players and coach stand together on the left. Place the two announcers in the middle. The Dragon team players and coach can stand together on the right. The students watching on the Chargers' side of the class can be Chargers' fans and the students on the Dragons' side can be Dragons' fans.

Props: You may wish to have the players on each team wear the same color shirts.

Presentation: The players can move their bodies as they act out the game.

Characters

Announcer One: 13 lines (2.7)
Announcer Two: 13 lines (2.1)

Charger One: 10 lines (1.9)
Charger Two: 10 lines (0.5)
Charger Three: 7 lines (0.5)
Charger Coach: 1 line (0.5)
Charger Fans: 15 lines (2.9)

Dragon One: 2 lines (2.4)
Dragon Two: 2 lines (2.0)
Dragon Goalie: 2 lines (3.2)
Dragon Fans: 15 lines (2.9)

First Point Soccer Readers Theatre Script

Announcer One:	It's Saturday morning and the entire park is filled with soccer games.
Announcer Two:	In the right corner of the park, the Chargers will be playing the Dragons.
Charger One:	I want to score the first goal of the game.
Charger Two:	It's always good to get ahead early.
Charger Three:	Get ahead and stay ahead.
Charger Coach:	That's the spirit! It's time for the game to start. Keep your eye on the ball after the kickoff.
Chargers:	Yes, Coach!
Announcer One:	All of the players are on the field for the kickoff.
Announcer Two:	The Dragons won the toss so they will kick the ball first.
Charger Fans:	Go Chargers!
Dragon Fans:	Go Dragons!
Announcer One:	Who will get the ball after the kickoff?
Announcer Two:	It looks like the Chargers have it now.
Charger One:	I got the ball. Now to make a goal.
Charger Two:	I'm right behind you!
Charger Three:	Let's go!
Charger Fans:	Go Chargers!
Dragon Fans:	Go Dragons!
Dragon One:	Not so fast.
Dragon Two:	We want to win this game!
Charger One:	You will have to catch me first!
Charger Fans:	Go Chargers!
Dragon Fans:	Go Dragons!
Announcer One:	The Chargers are charging across the field.
Announcer Two:	But the Dragons are on their tail.
Charger One:	There's the goal.
Charger Two:	Go for it!
Charger Fans:	Go Chargers!
Dragon Fans:	Go Dragons!
Announcer One:	The Chargers have kicked the ball.
Charger Fans:	Go Chargers!
Dragon Fans:	Go Dragons!
Announcer Two:	Will the Chargers make the first point of the game?
Dragon Goalie:	Got it!

From *Read and Write Sports: Readers Theatre and Writing Activities for Grades 3–8* by Anastasia Suen. Santa Barbara, CA: Libraries Unlimited. Copyright © 2011.

Announcer One:	The Dragon goalie has caught the ball.
Announcer Two:	No goal yet. The score is still Chargers zero, Dragons zero.
Charger Fans:	Go Chargers!
Dragon Fans:	Go Dragons!
Announcer One:	The Dragon goalie is making a goal kick.
Announcer Two:	Who will get the ball now?
Charger Fans:	Go Chargers!
Dragon Fans:	Go Dragons!
Charger Three:	I got it.
Charger Two:	Great!
Charger One:	Let's go!
Announcer One:	The Chargers have possession of the ball again.
Announcer Two:	They are living up to their name today!
Charger Fans:	Go Chargers!
Dragon Fans:	Go Dragons!
Charger Two:	Let's try that goal again.
Charger Three:	Get into position.
Charger One:	I'm ready, pass the ball.
Charger Two:	Here you go.
Dragon Two:	Not so fast.
Announcer One:	One of the Dragon players has taken possession of the ball.
Charger Fans:	Go Chargers!
Dragon Fans:	Go Dragons!
Announcer Two:	The Dragons are running across the field.
Charger Fans:	Go Chargers!
Dragon Fans:	Go Dragons!
Charger One:	That was my ball!
Dragon One:	We have it now.
Charger Two:	Not for long!
Announcer One:	The ball is loose.
Announcer Two:	Who will get possession of the ball this time?
Charger Fans:	Go Chargers!
Dragon Fans:	Go Dragons!
Announcer One:	The Chargers have taken back the ball.
Announcer Two:	They're running back to the other goal.
Charger Fans:	Go Chargers!
Dragon Fans:	Go Dragons!
Charger One:	I have to score a goal!

Charger Three:	We're right behind you.
Charger Two:	And so are the Dragons.
Charger Fans:	Go Chargers!
Dragon Fans:	Go Dragons!
Announcer One:	The Chargers have kicked the ball toward the goal.
Charger One:	Go in!
Charger Two:	Go in!
Charger Three:	Go in!
Announcer Two:	Can the Dragon goalie block it?
Charger Fans:	Go Chargers!
Dragon Fans:	Go Dragons!
Dragon Goalie:	NO!
Announcer One:	GOOOAALLLLLLLL!!!!!! The Chargers scored the first goal of the game.
Chargers:	Yeah!
Announcer Two:	The score is Chargers one, Dragons zero.
Charger Fans:	Go Chargers!
Dragon Fans:	Go Dragons!

Name Daniel   Date February 2

Soccer Topic Mind Map GO Chart

Write the name of your sport in the center circle and add details in the smaller circles.
This brainstorming will help you figure out a research question. What do you want to
know about this sport?

I want to know: Why do we call it soccer when others call it football?

From *Read and Write Sports: Readers Theatre and Writing Activities for Grades 3–8*
by Anastasia Suen. Santa Barbara, CA: Libraries Unlimited. Copyright © 2011.

Name Daniel   Date February 2

Soccer
Topic
ISP
GO Chart

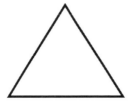

Find the answer to your sports research question with this ISP chart. Use short phrases to record your Information, Source, and Page.

I want to know: Why do we call it soccer when others call it football?

I: soccer called football or association football

S: World Book

P: http://www.worldbookonline.com/

I: word soccer comes from assoc. (abbreviation for association)

S: World Book

P: http://www.worldbookonline.com/

I: Football Association started in London in 1863

S: Encyclopaedia Britannica

P: http://www.britannica.com/EBchecked/topic/550852/football

I: U.S. Soccer Federation started in 1913

S: 2000 Olympics page

P: http://www.hellenism.com/olympics/ancientgames/javelin.htm

I: short name for association football (1889)

S: Merriam-Webster

P: http://www.merriam-webster.com/dictionary/soccer

Name Daniel   Date February 2

Soccer Topic Sandwich GO Chart

Organize the information from your ISP chart so you can write your sports paragraph.

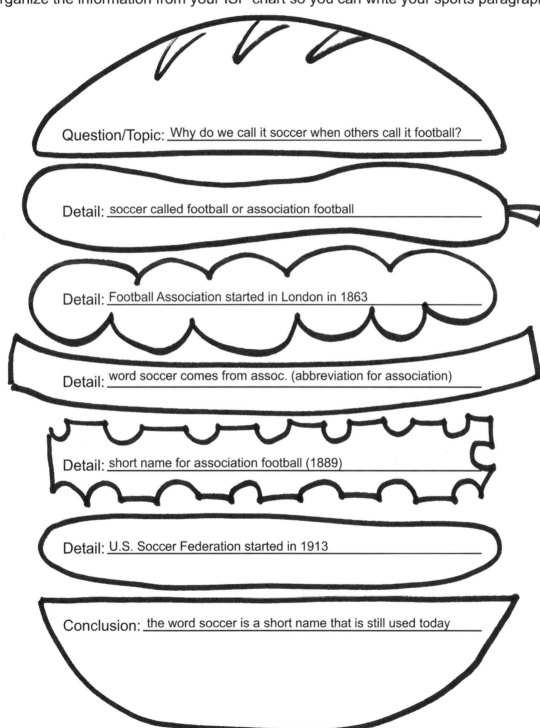

Question/Topic: Why do we call it soccer when others call it football?

Detail: soccer called football or association football

Detail: Football Association started in London in 1863

Detail: word soccer comes from assoc. (abbreviation for association)

Detail: short name for association football (1889)

Detail: U.S. Soccer Federation started in 1913

Conclusion: the word soccer is a short name that is still used today

From *Read and Write Sports: Readers Theatre and Writing Activities for Grades 3–8*
by Anastasia Suen. Santa Barbara, CA: Libraries Unlimited. Copyright © 2011.

Name Ashley   Date February 12

Soccer Scene Mind Map GO Chart

A scene is a small part of a longer story. It is over in a matter of minutes. What can
happen in just a few minutes when you play this sport? Write the sport in the center circle
and add details in the smaller circles. This will help you decide what aspect of this sport
you can write about today.

I want to write about: making a goal

Name Ashley   Date February 12

Soccer Scene Threes GO Chart

Real life goes on and on but a story starts when something changes. Your readers want to find out how someone solves a problem. Where is that person and what is the problem? Decide on the 3 essential elements of your scene. Use short phrases to record your decisions.

I want to write about: making a goal

To write a scene, you need 3 things:

a **PERSON:** number 9 on the Chargers team

in a **PLACE:** at a soccer match in the park

with a **PROBLEM:** wants to score a goal

Name **Ashley** _____ Date **February 12** _____

Soccer Scene Story Boxes (Step 1) GO Chart

Step 1: What happens during your scene? Write a short action phrase in each box.

game starts

kick ball

goal blocked

goalie kick

pass ball

stolen

stolen back

kick ball

Name Ashley   Date February 12

Soccer Scene Story Boxes (Step 2) GO Chart

Step 1: What happens during your scene? Write a short action phrase in each box.

listen to coach	**game starts**	start running
kick off		parents yell advice

chase ball	**kick ball**	dribble toward goal
trap ball		other players follow

Dragons goalie jumps	**goal blocked**	Dragons cheer
goalie catches ball		mad

ball goes into midfield	**goalie kick**	coach yells advice
Chargers get ball		parents yell advice

run down field	**pass ball**	dribble toward goal
trap ball		excited

tackled	**stolen**	run after them
run the other way		upset

I tackle	**stolen back**	run after it
ball gets loose		dribble ball to goal

Dragons goalie reaches	**kick ball**	I jump for joy
goalie misses		Chargers cheer

Step 2: Add 4 details (actions, descriptions, feelings) to each box.

From *Read and Write Sports: Readers Theatre and Writing Activities for Grades 3–8* by Anastasia Suen. Santa Barbara, CA: Libraries Unlimited. Copyright © 2011.

Name **Christopher**   Date **February 27**

Soccer Moment Mind Map GO Chart

A poem can capture a moment in time. What is happening in this sports moment? Write your sport in the center circle and add details in the smaller circles.

field
of players

ref running

parents
watching

Sport:
Soccer

kicking

soccer ball
on grass

dribbling

trapping

passing

I want to write about this moment in time: **dribbling the ball**

Name Christopher   Date February 27

Soccer Moment 6 Ws GO Chart

Answering the 6 Ws will help you write your sports moment poem.

I want to write about this moment in time: dribbling the ball

Who is the main character? me

What happens? I'm dribbling the ball across the field

When does it happen? during a soccer match

Where does it happen? at the park

Why does it happen? I want to make a goal

How does it happen?

　　　　Action: I dribble the ball across the field

　　　　Reaction: I get close to the goal, so I kick the ball

From *Read and Write Sports: Readers Theatre and Writing Activities for Grades 3–8*
by Anastasia Suen. Santa Barbara, CA: Libraries Unlimited. Copyright © 2011.

Soccer Moment Poetry Stretch

Add details to your 6 Ws and stretch your sports moment thoughts into a poem. Write your first draft below.

tap run

tap run

tap run

I dribble the soccer ball

across the grassy field

tap run

tap run

tap run

it's just like practice

we do this three times a week

tap run

tap run

tap run

but today is Saturday

so we're playing a game

tap run

tap run

tap run

and everything counts more

I've almost reached the goal

tap run

tap run

tap run

KICK!

Soccer Word Search

```
X C R O S S I N G P A S S F X C
Y J P P W I Q N O K H Y L F J S
E E G O A L I O X N T B U O R O
L G L V V S F N O L R E K K Q X
L R X K S F G I A E S Z M C E D
O A A A E P T N A N A S S I S T
V H P N U C E K E E X W Z K Z H
W C S K E P A F J Q Y Q Z B B U
N E F L S W E C W O R L D C U P
S Z F V A D E P R E V O N R U T
S E M Y C N E E R E F E R I O B
D N T L T Q E I M I R H C Z G G
D P J E L Z Z Z F Z C Q R C S P
T C R O W P A L R E V O U T O Z
O A A W K K C Q Q D R I B B L E
S T A E L C K N D R A W R O F I
```

assist	crossing pass	goal	penalty
breakaway	defense	kickoff	referee
center	deflection	offense	turnover
charge	dribble	overlap	volley
cleats	forward	passing	World Cup

Name_____ Date _____

Soccer Crossword Puzzle

ACROSS

3 Using your shoulder to push another player.

5 When a player stops the ball from going into the goal.

6 Sports shoes with bumps underneath.

9 Kicking the ball when it is still in the air.

10 Using your feet, legs or chest to stop the ball.

DOWN

1 To keep your body between the player and the ball.

2 Move the ball by tapping it with your feet.

4 Only the goalie can use this body part.

7 Using your feet or shoulder to take the ball away from another player.

8 Kick the ball away from your own goal.

From *Read and Write Sports: Readers Theatre and Writing Activities for Grades 3–8* by Anastasia Suen. Santa Barbara, CA: Libraries Unlimited. Copyright © 2011.

7

Track

Relay Race Track Readers Theatre Overview

Summary: At a district-wide track meet, 3 teams run a 400 meter relay race.

Readability: 2.6 for entire script (individual levels listed after each part)

Staging: From left to right, the announcer and the official, then the Haycox School team, the Curren School team and the Fremont School team. Have the players stand in racing order, behind their coach.

Props: You may wish to have the racers on each team pass the baton as they read that part of the play.

Presentation: The players can move their bodies as they act out the race.

Characters

> **Announcer**: 15 lines (3.4)
> **Official**: 9 lines (1.0)
> **Crowd**: 11 lines (3.4)
>
> **Haycox Coach**: 5 lines (0.2)
> **Haycox Racer One**: 5 lines (1.1)
> **Haycox Racer Two**: 6 lines (1.9)
> **Haycox Racer Three**: 5 lines (0.2)
> **Haycox Anchor**: 8 lines (0.0)
>
> **Curren Coach**: 3 lines (1.8)
> **Curren Racer One**: 4 lines (0.8)
> **Curren Racer Two**: 3 lines (1.3)
> **Curren Racer Three**: 3 lines (0.0)
> **Curren Anchor**: 3 lines (0.9)

Fremont Coach: 3 lines (0.3)
Fremont Racer One: 3 lines (3.4)
Fremont Racer Two: 3 lines (0.1)
Fremont Racer Three: 4 lines (1.0)
Fremont Anchor: 4 lines (1.3)

Relay Race Track Readers Theatre Script

Announcer:	It was Track and Field day for all the schools in the district. Everyone met at the big track at the high school.
Haycox Anchor:	I can't wait until it's time for the 400 meter relay.
Haycox Racer Three:	You get all the glory coming in last.
Haycox Anchor:	I can't win unless you're fast, too.
Haycox Racer One:	It takes all of us to win.
Haycox Racer Two:	That's right.
Haycox Coach:	It's almost time for the race.
Official:	Let's put the Haycox School team in lane one this year.
Haycox School Racers:	Go Haycox!
Official:	The Curren School team is in lane two.
Curren School Racers:	Go Curren!
Official:	The Fremont School team is in lane three.
Fremont School Racers:	Go Fremont!
Official:	Let's go around the track and get everyone set up. The first leg will stay here at the starting line.
Curren Coach:	The first leg of the race sets the pace.
Curren Racer One:	I'll run as fast as I can, Coach.
Announcer:	The three coaches and the rest of the racers walked to the exchange zone for the first handoff.
Official:	The racers for the second leg stand here.
Haycox Coach:	Here's your spot. Be ready for the handoff.
Haycox Racer Two:	I will, Coach.
Announcer:	Each leg of the race had its own exchange zone. The runner coming into the exchange zone would hand the baton to the runner waiting in the zone.
Official:	The third leg begins here.
Fremont Coach:	You're the halfway point in this race.
Fremont Racer Three:	I'll be careful with the baton, Coach.
Announcer:	The runner for the fourth leg of the relay was called the anchor. The anchor runner who crossed the finish line first was winning for the entire team.
Official:	And the anchor racers start here.
Haycox Coach:	In the end, it's up to you to win it.
Haycox Anchor:	I know, Coach, I'll run as fast as I can.
Curren Coach:	The handoff is very important.
Curren Anchor:	We've been practicing, Coach.
Fremont Coach:	Bring it home.

From Read and Write Sports: Readers Theatre and Writing Activities for Grades 3–8 by Anastasia Suen. Santa Barbara, CA: Libraries Unlimited. Copyright © 2011.

Fremont Anchor:	I'll give it my best, Coach.
Announcer:	The official and the coaches went back to the starting line.
Official:	On your mark, get set . . .
Haycox Racer One:	The race is starting!
Fremont Racer One:	I better get into position.
Curren Racer One:	I'm ready . . .
Curren Coach:	Keep your eyes on the runner.
Fremont Coach:	Watch the baton.
Haycox Coach:	Hit the baton hard to make sure the runner has it.
Announcer:	The official raised the starting pistol in the air.
Official:	BANG!
Crowd:	Go! Go! Go!
Announcer:	And the race is on. The first leg is 100 meters.
Crowd:	Go! Go! Go!
Announcer:	The Haycox School team is in the lead.
Crowd:	Go! Go! Go!
Announcer:	It's already time for the first handoff.
Haycox Racer One:	Here you go!
Haycox Racer Two:	I got it!
Fremont Racer One:	Here it is!
Fremont Racer Two:	Ready!
Curren Racer One:	We're already last.
Curren Racer Two:	I'll catch up.
Crowd:	Go! Go! Go!
Announcer:	Now the second leg is underway. They have 100 meters to run.
Crowd:	Go! Go! Go!
Announcer:	And then they'll hand off the baton again.
Crowd:	Go! Go! Go!
Haycox Racer Two:	We're in the lead.
Haycox Racer Three:	It'll stay that way!
Curren Racer Two:	Reach for it!!
Curren Racer Three:	I am, I am!
Fremont Racer Two:	We still have a ways to go.
Fremont Racer Three:	I got it!
Crowd:	Go! Go! Go!
Announcer:	Leg number three and another 100 meters to run.

Crowd:	Go! Go! Go!
Haycox Racer Three:	I'm almost there.
Haycox Anchor:	Just put in my hand!
Curren Racer Three:	We're catching up.
Curren Anchor:	I'll take care of it.
Fremont Racer Three:	We're losing them!
Fremont Anchor Racer:	I'm on it.
Crowd:	Go! Go! Go!
Announcer:	And now it's the anchor leg, the final 100 meters . . .
Crowd:	Go! Go! Go!
Announcer:	Whoever crosses the finish line first will win for their entire team.
Crowd:	Go! Go! Go!
Haycox Anchor:	There's the finish line.
Crowd:	Go! Go! Go!
Haycox Anchor:	I made it!
Announcer:	The Haycox School team has crossed the finish line first.
Haycox School Racers:	We won!

Name Elizabeth   Date March 2

Track Topic Mind Map GO Chart

Write the name of your sport in the center circle and add details in the smaller circles.
This brainstorming will help you figure out a research question. What do you want to
know about this sport?

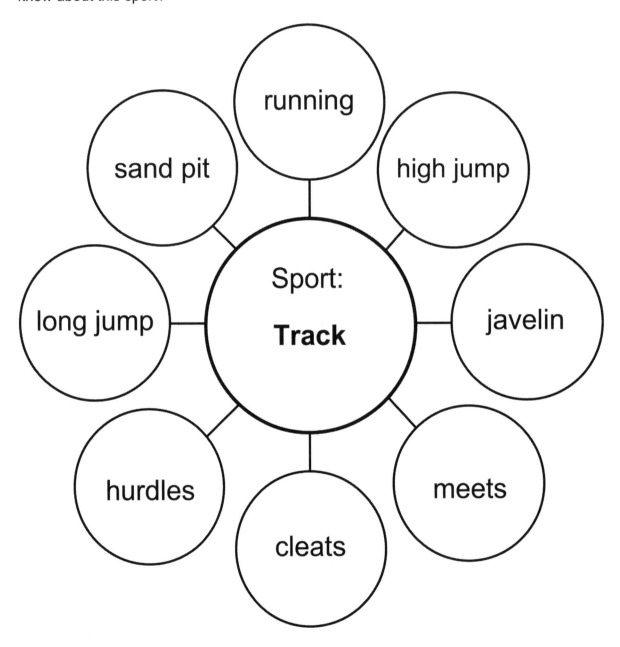

I want to know: Why do we have the javelin in track and field?

Name **Elizabeth**   Date **March 2**

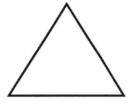

Track
Topic
ISP
GO Chart

Find the answer to your sports research question with this ISP chart. Use short phrases to record your Information, Source, and Page.

I want to know: **Why do we have the javelin in track and field?**

I: ancient weapon of war

S: World Book

P: http://www.worldbookonline.com/

I: one of 5 events in pentathlon

S: World Book

P: http://www.worldbookonline.com/

I: added to Olympics in 708 BC

S: World Book

P: http://www.worldbookonline.com/

I: used for war and hunting

S: 2000 Olympics page

P: http://www.hellenism.com/olympics/ancientgames/javelin.htm

I: included in the ancient Greek Olympic Games

S: Encyclopaedia Britannica

P: http://www.britannica.com/EBchecked/topic/301784/javelin-throw

From *Read and Write Sports: Readers Theatre and Writing Activities for Grades 3–8*
by Anastasia Suen. Santa Barbara, CA: Libraries Unlimited. Copyright © 2011.

Name **Elizabeth**   Date **March 2**

Track Topic Sandwich GO Chart

Organize the information from your ISP chart so you can write your sports paragraph.

Question/Topic: _Why do we have the javelin in track and field?_

Detail: _ancient weapon of war_

Detail: _used for war and hunting_

Detail: _one of 5 events in pentathlon_

Detail: _included in the ancient Greek Olympic Games_

Detail: _added to Olympics in 708 BC_

Conclusion: _one of the earliest Olympic track and field events_

Name <u>Anthony</u>   Date <u>March 19</u>

Track Scene Mind Map GO Chart

A scene is a small part of a longer story. It is over in a matter of minutes. What can happen in just a few minutes when you play this sport? Write the sport in the center circle and add details in the smaller circles. This will help you decide what aspect of this sport you can write about today.

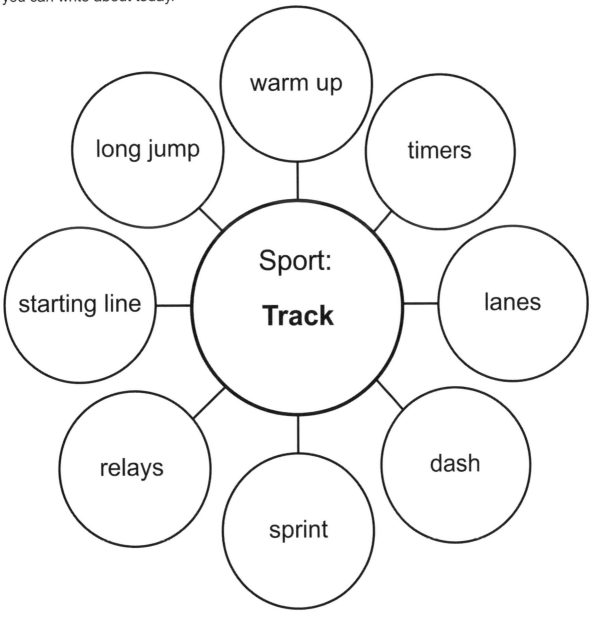

I want to write about: <u>running the 400 meter relay</u>

Name <u>Anthony</u>   Date <u>March 19</u>

Track Scene Threes GO Chart

Real life goes on and on but a story starts when something changes. Your readers want to find out how someone solves a problem. Where is that person and what is the problem? Decide on the 3 essential elements of your scene. Use short phrases to record your decisions.

I want to write about: <u>running the 400 meter relay</u>

To write a scene, you need 3 things:

a **PERSON:** <u>a runner wearing number 17</u>

in a **PLACE:** <u>at the 300 meter mark on the track</u>

with a **PROBLEM:** <u>needs the baton to run the final leg of the relay</u>

Name <u>Anthony</u>   Date <u>March 19</u>

Track Scene Story Boxes
(Step 1) GO Chart

Step 1: What happens during your scene? Write a short action phrase in each box.

assigned to a lane

go to 300 meter mark

hear starting gun

first runner

second runner

third runner

handoff

run

From *Read and Write Sports: Readers Theatre and Writing Activities for Grades 3–8* by Anastasia Suen. Santa Barbara, CA: Libraries Unlimited. Copyright © 2011.

Track Scene Story Boxes (Step 2) GO Chart

Step 1: What happens during your scene? Write a short action phrase in each box.

walk up to starting line	**assigned to a lane**	pin on number
official looks at clipboard		warm up
walk around the track	**go to 300 meter mark**	wave at family
look at crowd		watch official
get into position	**hear starting gun**	watch starting line
look at coach		yell encouragement
run down track	**first runner**	hold out baton for handoff
reach second runner		excited
arm back for handoff	**second runner**	run forward
grab baton		anxious
arm back for handoff	**third runner**	run forward
grab baton		jittery
arm back for handoff	**handoff**	run forward
grab baton		determined
pass other runners	**run**	crowd cheers
cross finish line first		pump arms in the air

Step 2: Add 4 details (actions, descriptions, feelings) to each box.

From *Read and Write Sports: Readers Theatre and Writing Activities for Grades 3–8* by Anastasia Suen. Santa Barbara, CA: Libraries Unlimited. Copyright © 2011.

Name **Samantha**   Date **March 25**

Track Moment Mind Map GO Chart

A poem can capture a moment in time. What is happening in this sports moment? Write your sport in the center circle and add details in the smaller circles.

on the track

dust

parents watching

Sport:

Track

crowd in bleachers

waiting to race

other runners warming up

coaches on sidelines

officials

I want to write about this moment in time: **waiting to race**

Name Samantha   Date March 25

Track Moment 6 Ws GO Chart

Answering the 6 Ws will help you write your sports moment poem.

I want to write about this moment in time: waiting to race

Who is the main character? me

What happens? I'm standing at the starting line

When does it happen? during a meet

Where does it happen? on the track

Why does it happen? my turn to race

How does it happen?

    Action: I hear the starting gun

    Reaction: I start running

Name <u>Samantha</u>   Date <u>March 25</u>

Track Moment Poetry Stretch

Add details to your 6 Ws and stretch your sports moment thoughts into a poem. Write your first draft below.

<u>We talk</u>

<u>We stretch</u>

<u>We wait</u>

<u>The official walks over</u>

<u>And lifts her arm</u>

<u>Onto the blocks I go</u>

<u>Hands forward</u>

<u>Feet back</u>

<u>Waiting</u>

<u>Waiting</u>

<u>BANG!</u>

<u>We're off!</u>

Track Word Search

```
S R V T N M N I L E V A J A W E T
G E E P M U J G N O L O B I Y M R
K P N G B S R E V O E G N A H C W
X P A A W K S E L C H R S S K U S
Q E A L L R K G G Y A L E R D I T
H N D E C A T H L O N A F B C E U
E T B T V M H V T D W A O G T N P
P A K R S R H C M W G S D J N O T
T T P A E U T L U A V E L O P Z O
A H M T L O K H A O D C H J J E H
T L U S D Y S O A T R T V Z H G S
H O J E R N T Y P Z A C E H I N X
L N H S U O A H G R Q Z Z A G A J
O S G L H L R N A R O H C N A H A
N H I A E L T M G L I X X A B C U
A D H F D Z B R E A K L I N E X H
I N U G S R E T R A T S W L W E I
```

anchor	heptathlon	on your mark
breakline	high jump	pentathlon
changeover	hurdles	pole vault
crouch	javelin	relay
decathlon	lanes	shot put
exchange zone	long jump	starter's gun
false start	marathon	

From *Read and Write Sports: Readers Theatre and Writing Activities for Grades 3–8* by Anastasia Suen. Santa Barbara, CA: Libraries Unlimited. Copyright © 2011.

Track Crossword Puzzle

ACROSS
3 The last runner in a relay race.
5 One time around the track.
6 Four runners work as team, running one after the other.
7 The starter's second command to the runners.
8 Early race to determine who advances to the finals.
9 Eight areas on the track for the runners.
10 A pistol that shoots blanks to start the race.

DOWN
1 A short race run at full speed.
2 A runner begins before the starter's gun is fired.
4 Passing the baton from one runner to the next.

8

Gymnastics

I Can Do That! Gymnastics Readers Theatre Overview

Summary: A group of children enjoy a gymnastics birthday party at a gym.

Readability: 1.9 for entire script (individual levels listed after each part)

Staging: From left to right, the narrator, the two coaches and then the party guests in number order. The "Party Guests" lines are for the guests with speaking parts and the rest of the class watching the play.

Props: You may wish to allow Guests One to Eight to take off their shoes and socks and place them on the floor at one side of the room during the play.

Presentation: The players can move their bodies as they act out the play.

Characters

> **Narrator**: 12 lines (3.3)
> **Party Guests**: 15 lines (1.3)
>
> **Coach One**: 10 lines (0.3)
> **Coach Two**: 10 lines (0.7)
>
> **Guest One**: 1 line (2.5)
> **Guest Two**: 2 lines (0.6)
> **Guest Three**: 1 line (1.4)
> **Guest Four**: 1 line (1.3)
> **Guest Five**: 1 line (3.0)
> **Guest Six**: 1 line (3.0)
> **Guest Seven**: 2 lines (2.2)
> **Guest Eight**: 2 lines (1.0)

I Can Do That! Gymnastics Readers Theatre Script

Narrator: The guests were arriving for a birthday party at Jamba's Gym. Everyone was talking at once.

Party Guests: Talk, talk, talk!

Guest One: Have you ever been here before?

Guest Two: I practice here three times a week.

Party Guests: Talk, talk, talk!

Coach One: It's two o'clock, time to get this party started!

Party Guests: Talk, talk, talk!

Coach Two: I want everyone to take off their shoes and socks and put them over there in the cubbies.

Guest Three: Why can't we wear our socks?

Coach One: Your socks might get lost in the foam pit.

Party Guests: Ooooo, the foam pit!

Coach Two: Over there . . .

Party Guests: Can we do that now?

Coach One: First we have stretch and warm up.

Coach Two: Come over to the mat so we can start.

Narrator: The two coaches led all of the Party Guests through a stretching routine.

Party Guests: Stretch, stretch, stretch!

Coach One: Now line up at the edge of the mat.

Coach Two: We'll start with something easy.

Narrator: The coach does a forward roll, also called a somersault.

Party Guests: I can do that!

Coach One: Good! Everyone will get a turn.

Coach Two: You go first.

Guest Four: Me? Uh, okay . . .

Guest Five: My turn.

Guest Six: Now me.

Narrator: All of the party guests did a forward roll.

Party Guests: What can we do now?

Coach One: Let's try the balance beam.

Coach Two: Come this way.

Narrator: The party guests walked in the line over to the balance beam. One balance beam was on the mat on the floor. The other balance beam had legs so it was up in the air.

Coach One: We will start with the low one first.

Party Guests:	I can do that!
Narrator:	One by one, each party guest walked on the low balance beam.
Party Guests:	That was so easy.
Coach Two:	Now let's try the higher one.
Party Guests:	How do we get up there?
Coach One:	I'll help you.
Guest Seven:	I don't want to fall.
Coach Two:	I'll walk next to you.
Guest Seven:	I made it!
Narrator:	After everyone had a turn, it was time for the rings.
Guest Eight:	How do I get up there?
Coach One:	I'll lift you up.
Coach Two:	Grab the rings.
Guest Eight:	Oh, my arms! This is harder than it looks.
Narrator:	After everyone had a turn on the rings, it was time for the trampoline.
Party Guests:	The trampoline!
Narrator:	The coaches gave instructions.
Coach One:	After you jump a few times on the trampoline, land in the foam pit.
Party Guests:	The foam pit!
Coach Two:	Then get back in line so the next person can jump.
Narrator:	One by one the Party Guests jumped on the trampoline.
Party Guests:	Jump, jump, jump . . .
Narrator:	Up in the air and into the foam pit.
Party Guests:	Again, again!
Narrator:	And so that's what they did.

Name William   Date April 5

Gymnastics Topic Mind Map
GO Chart

Write the name of your sport in the center circle and add details in the smaller circles.
This brainstorming will help you figure out a research question. What do you want to
know about this sport?

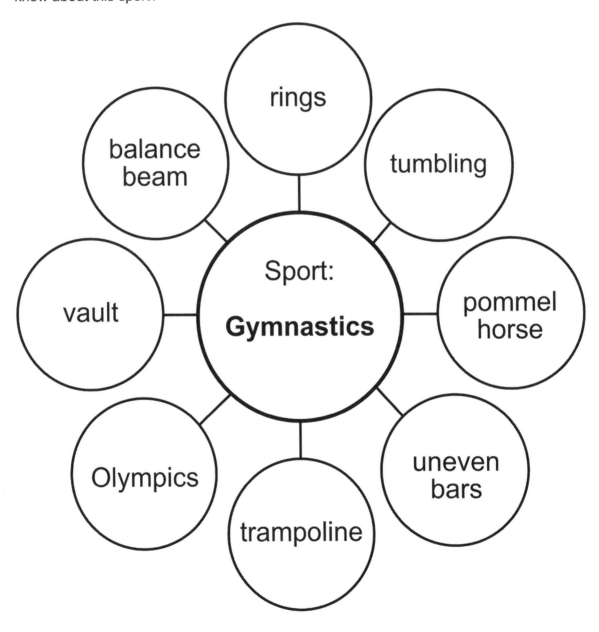

I want to know: When was the trampoline invented?

Name William   Date April 5

Gymnastics
Topic
ISP
GO Chart

Find the answer to your sports research question with this ISP chart. Use short phrases to record your Information, Source, and Page.

I want to know: When was the trampoline invented?

I: gymnast George Nissen perfected it (1936)

S: Encyclopaedia Britannica

P: http://www.britannica.com/EBchecked/topic/602236/trampoline

I: first performed in circus

S: Encyclopaedia Britannica

P: http://www.britannica.com/EBchecked/topic/602236/trampoline

I: circus acts gave him the idea

S: Acrobatic Sports

P: http://www.acrobaticsports.com/detail.do?noArticle=1863&id_key=309

I: Nissen made first one at age 16 (1930)

S: New York Times

P: http://www.nytimes.com/2010/04/13/us/13nissen.html?_r=1

I: name is Spanish word for diving board (with extra e at end)

S: New York Times

P: http://www.nytimes.com/2010/04/13/us/13nissen.html?_r=1

Name William   Date April 5

Gymnastics Topic Sandwich
GO Chart

Organize the information from your ISP chart so you can write your sports paragraph.

Question/Topic: When was the trampoline invented?

Detail: Nissen made first one at age 16 (1930)

Detail: circus acts gave him the idea

Detail: first performed in circus

Detail: gymnast George Nissen perfected it (1936)

Detail: name is Spanish word for diving board (with extra e at end)

Conclusion: George Nissan created the first trampoline at age 16 and after he perfected it, he began touring with it in the circus

Name Isabella   Date April 13

Gymnastics Scene Mind Map
GO Chart

A scene is a small part of a longer story. It is over in a matter of minutes. What can happen in just a few minutes when you play this sport? Write the sport in the center circle and add details in the smaller circles. This will help you decide what aspect of this sport you can write about today.

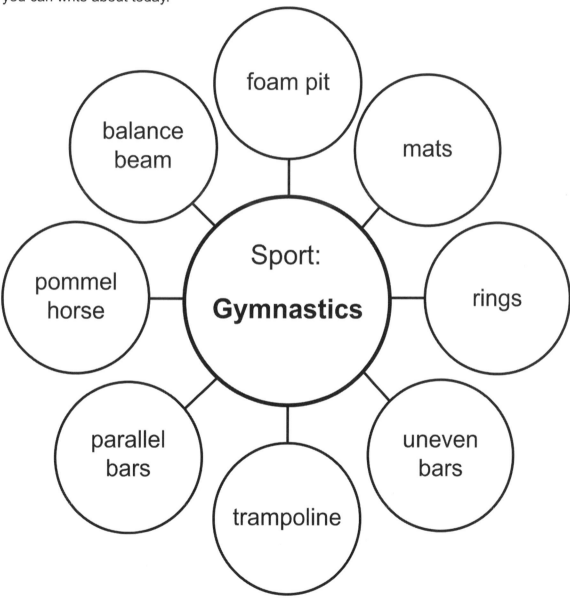

I want to write about: a gymnastics birthday party

Gymnastics Scene Threes
GO Chart

Real life goes on and on but a story starts when something changes. Your readers want to find out how someone solves a problem. Where is that person and what is the problem? Decide on the 3 essential elements of your scene. Use short phrases to record your decisions.

I want to write about: a gymnastics birthday party

To write a scene, you need 3 things:

a PERSON: a party guest

in a PLACE: at a birthday party at a gymnastics gym

with a PROBLEM: trying to use the gymnastics equipment

From *Read and Write Sports: Readers Theatre and Writing Activities for Grades 3–8* by Anastasia Suen. Santa Barbara, CA: Libraries Unlimited. Copyright © 2011.

Name **Isabella**   Date **April 13**

Gymnastics Scene Story Boxes (Step 1) GO Chart

Step 1: What happens during your scene? Write a short action phrase in each box.

stretching

tumbling

balance beam

rings

trampoline

foam pit

Gymnastics Scene Story Boxes (Step 2) GO Chart

Step 1: What happens during your scene? Write a short action phrase in each box.

at gymnastics gym	**stretching**	coach gives directions
birthday party		friends talking

all line up	**tumbling**	cartwheel
somersault		laughing

low one easy	**balance beam**	almost fall off
higher one harder		embarrassing

coach lifts me up	**rings**	arms ache
try to lift legs		let go

jumping	**trampoline**	don't want to stop
fun		others say hurry up

jump in	**foam pit**	want to do it again!
land		happy

Step 2: Add 4 details (actions, descriptions, feelings) to each box.

Name **Nicholas**   Date **April 27**

Gymnastics Moment Mind Map
GO Chart

A poem can capture a moment in time. What is happening in this sports moment? Write
your sport in the center circle and add details in the smaller circles.

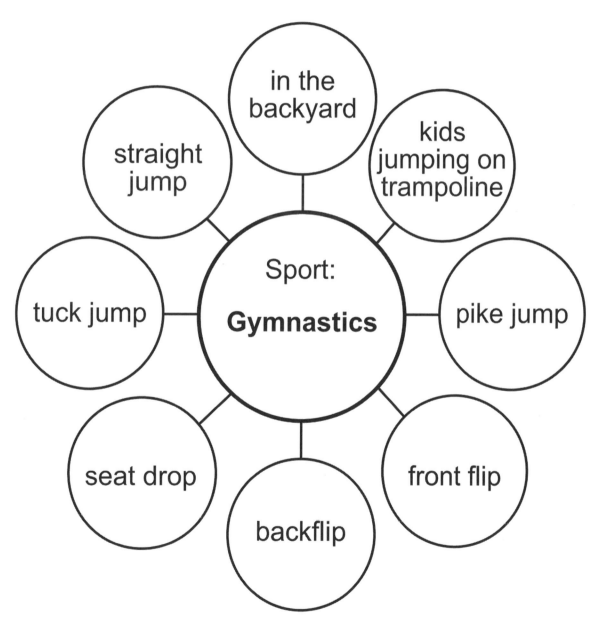

- in the backyard
- kids jumping on trampoline
- straight jump
- pike jump
- tuck jump

Sport:

Gymnastics

- seat drop
- front flip
- backflip

I want to write about this moment in time: **doing a backflip**

Name Nicholas   Date April 27

Gymnastics Moment 6 Ws
GO Chart

Answering the 6 Ws will help you write your sports moment poem.

I want to write about this moment in time: doing a backflip

Who is the main character? me

What happens? I do a backflip

When does it happen? on the weekend

Where does it happen? on the trampoline

Why does it happen? my turn to use the trampoline

How does it happen?

Action: I jump higher and higher

Reaction: I flip over

Name **Nicholas**   Date **April 27**

Gymnastics Moment Poetry Stretch

Add details to your 6 Ws and stretch your sports moment thoughts into a poem. Write your first draft below.

my turn at last

I climb onto the trampoline

and jump

higher

higher

higher

do something

they yell

we'll film it

Okay

I say

I jump up

higher

higher

higher

I flip my legs

up and over my head

backflip!

Gymnastics Word Search

```
W Z D E X Z N O P T I O N A L S Z
O O T L A S Q S E T T E U O R I P
L T U C K D F F O D N U O R H I Z
Y S E D E D U C T I O N M R I Y F
M D O N F G Q M A X S G A K O F W
P N C O X V N M J R X M P F H F N
I U O I C R H I H X B P L D Q T T
C O M T F L O O R E X E R C I S E
O R P U E S W Z P P X M U R A I A
R A U C A W U S P I S E N E I W A
D L L E T O R T B B A D C L U T F
E L S X W L Z I A E X Z N E Q A V
R A O E H C L T R R I L T A C T V
L S R R O I L I O E A T R S H R S
K Q I A T U A C I F C P V E G Y X
W E E Y A L M Q J A R Y P K Q F X
Z T S V I Q U N E V E N B A R S U
```

aerial	floor exercise	salto
all arounds	handspring	tuck
apparatus	Olympic order	twist
compulsories	optionals	uneven bars
deduction	pirouettes	vault
execution	release	
flexibility	round off	

 From *Read and Write Sports: Readers Theatre and Writing Activities for Grades 3–8* by Anastasia Suen. Santa Barbara, CA: Libraries Unlimited. Copyright © 2011.

Name_____ Date _____

Gymnastics Crossword Puzzle

ACROSS

2 A score for all of the events at a competition.
6 A piece of equipment used in competition.
7 A skill performed without hands touching the equipment or the ground.
9 Required routines each gymnast must perform.
10 Two bars at different heights.

DOWN

1 A routine performed to music on a large mat.
3 A combination of stunts performed on one piece of equipment.
4 The order of events in the Olympics.
5 Personal routines created by the gymnast.
8 Letting go.

9

BMX

Second Moto BMX Readers Theatre Overview

Summary: Five bicycle riders compete in a BMX race.

Readability: 2.9 for entire script (individual levels listed after each part)

Staging: From left to right, the two announcers, the official, and the five racers in racing order by lane: #3, #5, #12, #20, and #7.

Props: You may wish to allow the racers to wear bicycle helmets.

Presentation: The players can move their bodies as they act out the race.

Characters

> **Announcer One**: 8 lines (3.9)
> **Announcer Two**: 8 lines (3.4)
> **Official**: 1 line (0.5)
> **Crowd**: 8 lines (3.4)
>
> **Racer Number 3**: 6 lines (0.2)
> **Racer Number 5**: 6 lines (0.5)
> **Racer Number 7**: 6 lines (1.3)
> **Racer Number 12**: 8 lines (0.7)
> **Racer Number 20**: 6 lines (0.6)

Second Moto BMX Readers Theatre Script

Announcer One:	Every BMX racer competes in three races called motos.
Announcer Two:	After the first moto, all the racers will compete with each other again in the second moto.
Announcer One:	For each race, the riders are assigned a lane at the starting gate.
Announcer Two:	The lane assignments for each race are posted on the moto board.
Racer Number 12:	I'm in lane three this time.
Racer Number 7:	Lane five for me.
Racer Number 20:	I'm in lane four.
Racer Number 5:	Lane two is mine.
Racer Number 3:	I'm in lane one. Lane one is for winners.
Racer Number 12:	You wish!
Announcer One:	Before the race, the riders gather in a staging area to wait their turn.
Announcer Two:	After the riders at the gate start racing, the next group lines up.
Official:	We're ready for the next group.
Announcer One:	The racing gate is pulled back up.
Announcer Two:	Each rider gets into their assigned lane.
Racer Number 3:	I have to get my pedal in the right spot.
Racer Number 5:	Let me adjust this mouthpiece.
Racer Number 20:	This helmet strap is too loose.
Racer Number 7:	Hi, Mom! Hi, Dad!
Racer Number 12:	I have to win this race . . .
Announcer One:	When the gate drops, the race is on!
Crowd:	Go! Go! Go!
Announcer Two:	The racers ride over the starting gate and down the first hill.
Crowd:	Go! Go! Go!
Announcer One:	After the straightaway, the riders come to the first turn.
Crowd:	Go! Go! Go!
Racer Number 5:	Turning left . . .
Racer Number 20:	Now's my chance to make the move.
Racer Number 12:	I have to pass these other bikes.
Racer Number 3:	Around the corner . . .
Racer Number 7:	Hey, wait for me!
Announcer Two:	There are three large hills coming up next.
Crowd:	Go! Go! Go!

Racer Number 20: This is my favorite part.

Racer Number 12: Up and over.

Racer Number 5: I'm flying!

Racer Number 7: Hang on tight!

Racer Number 3: One, two, three.

Announcer One: The racers are coming into the second turn.

Crowd: Go! Go! Go!

Racer Number 5: Turning right . . .

Racer Number 12: I still have to pass another bike.

Racer Number 20: Watch out!

Race Number 3: You almost hit me!

Racer Number 7: I'm pedaling as fast as I can.

Announcer Two: The rhythm section is next. There are seven small hills in a row.

Crowd: Go! Go! Go!

Racer Number 12: This is my last chance.

Racer Number 5: Hey, don't pass me up!

Racer Number 20: Up and down, up and down, up and down . . .

Racer Number 7: Whoops!

Race Number 3: I have to catch up.

Narrator One: The riders are just yards away from the finish line.

Crowd: Go! Go! Go!

Narrator Two: Who will win this moto?

Crowd: Go! Go! Go!

Racer Number 12: I won!

Name **Ryan**   Date **May 12**

BMX Topic Mind Map GO Chart

Write the name of your sport in the center circle and add details in the smaller circles. This brainstorming will help you figure out a research question. What do you want to know about this sport?

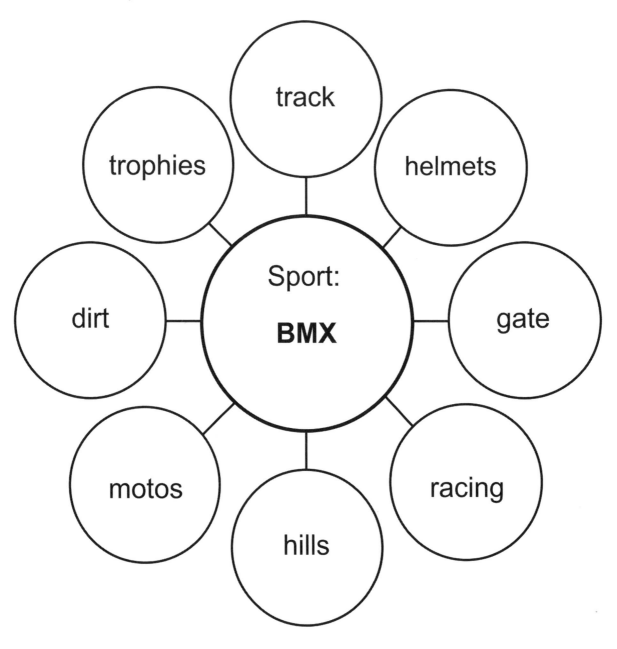

I want to know: **Why is it called BMX?**

Name Ryan   Date May 12

BMX
Topic
ISP
GO Chart

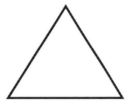

Find the answer to your sports research question with this ISP chart. Use short phrases to record your Information, Source, and Page.

I want to know: Why is it called BMX?

I: BMX is bicycle motocross

S: World Book

P: http://www.worldbookonline.com/

I: 4 kinds of bicycle races

S: World Book

P: http://www.worldbookonline.com/

I: cross-country races are outdoors in fields and hills

S: World Book

P: http://www.worldbookonline.com/

I: moto is for motorcycle and cross is for cross-country

S: Merriam-Webster Dictionary

P: http://www.merriam-webster.com/dictionary/motocross

I: motocross racing has steep hills and turns

S: Encarta Dictionary

P: http://encarta.msn.com/dictionary

Name Ryan   Date May 12

BMX Topic Sandwich GO Chart

Organize the information from your ISP chart so you can write your sports paragraph.

Question/Topic: Why is it called BMX?

Detail: 4 kinds of bicycle races

Detail: BMX is bicycle motocross

Detail: moto is for motorcycle and cross is for cross-country

Detail: motocross racing has steep hills and turns

Detail: cross-country races are outdoors in fields and hills

Conclusion: BMX is cross-country racing with bicycles

Name Grace   Date May 17

BMX Scene Mind Map GO Chart

A scene is a small part of a longer story. It is over in a matter of minutes. What can
happen in just a few minutes when you play this sport? Write the sport in the center circle
and add details in the smaller circles. This will help you decide what aspect of this sport
you can write about today.

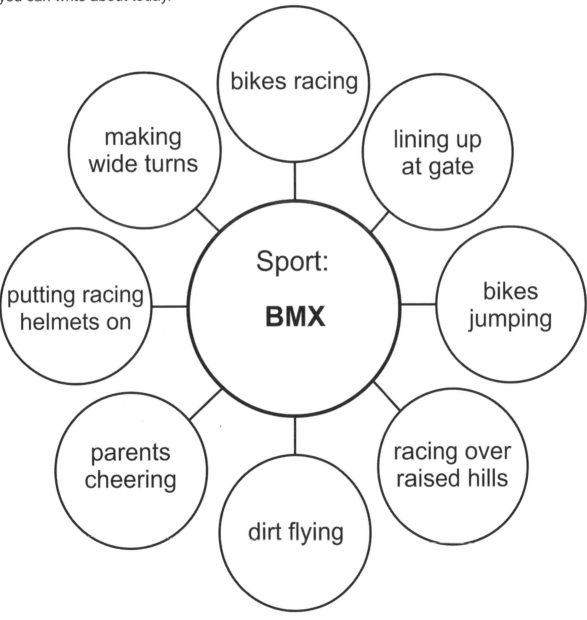

I want to write about: a race

From *Read and Write Sports: Readers Theatre and Writing Activities for Grades 3–8*
by Anastasia Suen. Santa Barbara, CA: Libraries Unlimited. Copyright © 2011.

BMX Scene Threes GO Chart

Real life goes on and on but a story starts when something changes. Your readers want to find out how someone solves a problem. Where is that person and what is the problem? Decide on the 3 essential elements of your scene. Use short phrases to record your decisions.

I want to write about: a race

To write a scene, you need 3 things:

a **PERSON:** a rider wearing number 12

in a **PLACE:** at the starting line of a BMX race

with a **PROBLEM:** has to win this race to qualify for the final

Name Grace   Date May 17

BMX Scene Story Boxes
(Step 1) GO Chart

Step 1: What happens during your scene? Write a short action phrase in each box.

ride up to starting gate

ride down first ramp

go into first turn

jump three hills

go into second turn

ride small hills

cross finish line

From *Read and Write Sports: Readers Theatre and Writing Activities for Grades 3–8*
by Anastasia Suen. Santa Barbara, CA: Libraries Unlimited. Copyright © 2011.

BMX Scene Story Boxes (Step 2) GO Chart

Step 1: What happens during your scene? Write a short action phrase in each box.

| look at other riders | ride up to starting gate | get pedals ready for start |
| tighten helmet strap | | watch official |

| gate drops | ride down first ramp | pedal quickly |
| race is on! | | excited |

| ride low on track | go into first turn | watch out for other riders |
| lean into turn | | go around first crash |

| ride out of turn | jump three hills | hold handlebars steady |
| pedal quickly | | land hard |

| pedal quickly | go into second turn | pass another rider |
| lean into the turn | | determined |

| hold handlebars steady | ride small hills | pass two riders |
| ride and jump four times | | excited |

| pedal as fast as possible | cross finish line | pass one more rider |
| go down straightaway | | I won! |

| | | |
| | | |

Step 2: Add 4 details (actions, descriptions, feelings) to each box.

Name David   Date May 23

BMX Moment Mind Map GO Chart

A poem can capture a moment in time. What is happening in this sports moment? Write your sport in the center circle and add details in the smaller circles.

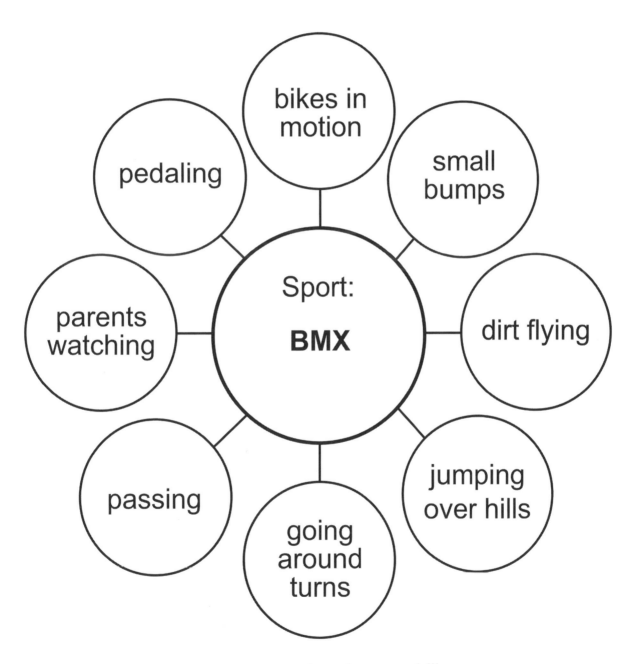

I want to write about this moment in time: jumping over hills

From *Read and Write Sports: Readers Theatre and Writing Activities for Grades 3–8* by Anastasia Suen. Santa Barbara, CA: Libraries Unlimited. Copyright © 2011.

141

Name <u>David</u>   Date <u>May 23</u>

BMX Moment 6 Ws GO Chart

Answering the 6 Ws will help you write your sports moment poem.

I want to write about this moment in time: <u>jumping over hills</u>

Who is the main character? <u>me</u>

What happens? <u>ride bike up to the hill</u>

When does it happen? <u>during a race</u>

Where does it happen? <u>on the track</u>

Why does it happen? <u>my turn to race</u>

Ho**w** does it happen?

    Action: <u>I ride up to the hill</u>

    Reaction: <u>I ride over it and jump the bike into the air</u>

Name David   Date May 23

BMX Moment Poetry Stretch

Add details to your 6 Ws and stretch your sports moment thoughts into a poem. Write your first draft below.

there's the next hill

I pedal

I pedal

I pedal

up the hill

and over

the top

into the air

I'm flying!

BMX Word Search

```
R H Y T H M S E C T I O N W Y D
S W E T A G G N I T R A T S J Y
S P B R A K E S E L D D A S T F
G L S T A G I N G A R E A M R I
T N A M O T O K V T I B X P E L
P J M N P I S F N D W A S Z P A
G E A G O W H E A X A S X D X U
H W T P E I V N O V I C E J E Q
O K E U X E T E K C O R P S F S
S B U U N G I A P T A V S X B I
T P R I G N I D N A L B T J S D
R P A W C K W F B D A L L K G K
I M V F I N I S H J N Y N E Q B
D I Q N I A H C H H N A A S S Z
E I G N T N A S I Q R R R Z U J
R T I H E L M E T C Q C Z G U X
```

amateur	expert	main event	starting gate
brakes	finish	moto	sprocket
cables	ghost rider	novice	
chain	grand nationals	rhythm section	
cranks	helmet	saddle	
disqualify	landing	staging area	

From Read and Write Sports: Readers Theatre and Writing Activities for Grades 3–8 by Anastasia Suen. Santa Barbara, CA: Libraries Unlimited. Copyright © 2011.

Name_____ Date_____

BMX Crossword Puzzle

ACROSS
2 Plastic cover over the handlebars.
5 Extra points given for attending national BMX events.
6 A jump on the track that is flat on top.
7 The chainwheel on a bicycle.
9 The wheel revolves on this shaft.

DOWN
1 One race.
3 An area of the track with several small jumps in a row.
4 Two pronged part of the frame that holds the wheel.
7 The bicycle seat.
8 L-shaped metal arm that holds the pedal.

10

Skateboarding

Saturday Afternoon Skateboarding Readers Theatre Overview

Summary: Three friends try skateboard tricks on the curb and a crowd gathers to watch.

Readability: 4.0 for entire script (individual levels listed after each part)

Staging: From left to right, the three narrators and the three skateboarders.

Props: You may wish to allow the three skateboarders to wear protective gear, such as a helmet and elbow and knee pads.

Presentation: The players can move their bodies as they act out the skateboard tricks.

Characters

> **Narrator One**: 7 lines (5.3)
> **Narrator Two**: 6 lines (3.5)
> **Narrator Three**: 6 lines (2.9)
>
> **Skateboarder One**: 10 lines (0.7)
> **Skateboarder Two**: 11 lines (0.0)
> **Skateboarder Three**: 10 lines (0.4)
>
> **Crowd**: 15 lines (2.7)

Saturday Afternoon Skateboarding Readers Theatre Script

Narrator One:	It was a quiet Saturday afternoon, perfect for skateboarding.
Skateboarder One:	No one's around, we can skate here.
Skateboarder Two:	Ready to ride?
Skateboarder Three:	Yes, I'm ready.
Skateboarder One:	This curb needs more wax.
Narrator Two:	If there are too many bumps in the curb, it slows the skateboard down.
Narrator Three:	Adding wax to the curb smoothes out the bumps so the skateboard slides over it more smoothly.
Skateboarder One:	There, that looks better.
Skateboarder Two:	Just right for grinding.
Skateboarder Three:	Let me show you how it's done.
Narrator One:	Some of the kids from the neighborhood came over to watch.
Skateboarder One:	You, show me?
Skateboarder Three:	Yes, make room for master.
Skateboarder Two:	Since when are you a skateboarding master?
Skateboarder One:	Show me what you can do then. Can you do an ollie like this?
Narrator One:	To do an ollie, you push down on the back of the skateboard with one foot.
Narrator Two:	The skateboard pops up into the air and you jump up with it.
Narrator Three:	Then gravity takes over, and you and your skateboard come back to earth.
Crowd:	Oooh!
Skateboarder Two:	It's all right, now watch this. Pop-jump-land.
Crowd:	Aaah!
Skateboarder Three:	Watch the master at work.
Crowd:	Yeah!
Narrator One:	Everyone could do the ollie, so it was time for another trick.
Skateboarder Three:	And here's a caveman.
Narrator Two:	To do a caveman, you throw your board into the air.
Narrator Three:	Then you jump up and land on the board before it hits the ground.
Crowd:	Oooh!
Skateboarder One:	Of course I can do that.
Crowd:	Aaah!

Skateboarder Two:	I can do it, too.
Crowd:	Yeah!
Narrator One:	Everyone could do that trick, too, so it was time to try something else.
Skateboarder Two:	The curb is waxed, so I'll do a frontside 50-50 grind.
Narrator Two:	The frontside 50-50 grind begins with an ollie.
Narrator Three:	After you pop your board onto the curb, you slide across it.
Crowd:	Oooh!
Skateboarder Three:	Watch me grind.
Crowd:	Aaah!
Skateboarder One:	It's my wax, so of course I can do a 50-50 grind.
Crowd:	Yeah!
Skateboarder One:	But can you do a manual like this?
Narrator One:	A manual is a wheelie on a skateboard.
Narrator Two:	You ride on the back of the board.
Narrator Three:	The front wheels are up in the air.
Crowd:	Oooh!
Skateboarder Two:	That's a little harder, but I can do it.
Crowd:	Aaah!
Skateboarder Three:	I can do that, too.
Crowd:	Yeah!
Skateboarder Three:	I can do it on the curb too.
Skateboarder Two:	A 5-0 grind? Let's see it.
Crowd:	Uh-oh!
Narrator One:	The skateboard wobbled and fell off the curb.
Skateboarder Three:	Well, I almost did it.
Skateboarder Two:	Let me try.
Crowd:	Oh, no!
Narrator Two:	The skateboard landed on the curb after the ollie.
Narrator Three:	And then the board flew off into the bushes! Ouch!
Skateboarder Two:	That's harder than it looks.
Skateboarder One:	My turn.
Crowd:	Oooh! Aaah! Yeah!
Skateboarder One:	Yes! I did it!
Skateboarder Two:	Pound it!
Skateboarder Three:	Pound it!

Name Alyssa   Date June 3

Skateboarding Topic Mind Map
GO Chart

Write the name of your sport in the center circle and add details in the smaller circles. This brainstorming will help you figure out a research question. What do you want to know about this sport?

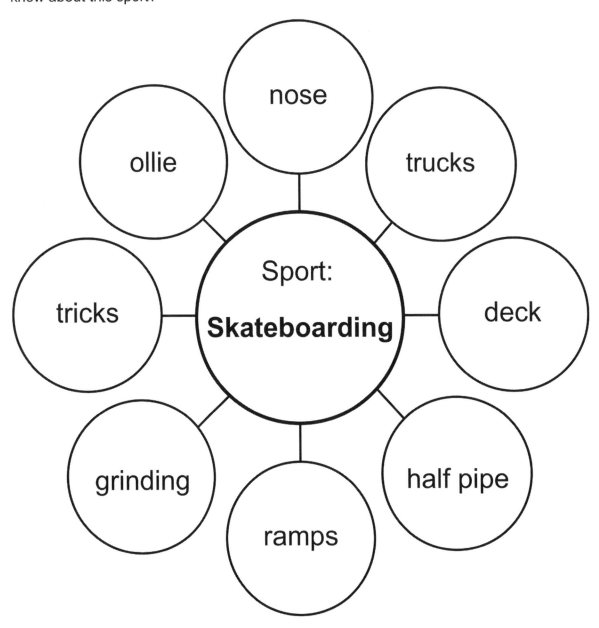

I want to know: When was skateboarding invented?

Name _Alyssa_____ Date _June 3_____

Skateboarding
Topic
ISP
GO Chart

Find the answer to your sports research question with this ISP chart. Use short phrases to record your Information, Source, and Page.

I want to know: _When was skateboarding invented?_____

I: _started with scooters made of wooden crates in 1920s_____

S: _World Book_____

P: _http://www.worldbookonline.com/_____

I: _two-by-four wood with roller skate wheels_____

S: _kidzworld_____

P: _http://www.kidzworld.com/article/6543-great-moments-in-skateboarding-history_

I: _called "sidewalk surfing" in 1960s_____

S: _Encyclopaedia Britannica_____

P: _http://www.britannica.com/EBchecked/topic/547332/skateboarding_

I: _first commercial skateboards in 1959 (sold in stores)_____

S: _Encyclopaedia Britannica_____

P: _http://www.britannica.com/EBchecked/topic/547332/skateboarding_

I: _roller skate wheels attached to surfboards_____

S: _The Encyclopedia of North American Sports History_____

P: _http://www.fofweb.com/_____

Name Alyssa   Date June 3

Skateboarding Topic Sandwich
GO Chart

Organize the information from your ISP chart so you can write your sports paragraph.

Question/Topic: When was skateboarding invented?

Detail: started with scooters made of wooden crates in 1920s

Detail: two-by-four wood with roller skate wheels

Detail: roller skate wheels attached to surfboards

Detail: first commercial skateboards in 1959 (sold in stores)

Detail: called "sidewalk surfing" in 1960s

Conclusion: skateboarding started in the 1920s and changed over time

Name <u>Tyler</u>   Date <u>June 5</u>

Skateboarding Scene Mind Map GO Chart

A scene is a small part of a longer story. It is over in a matter of minutes. What can happen in just a few minutes when you play this sport? Write the sport in the center circle and add details in the smaller circles. This will help you decide what aspect of this sport you can write about today.

I want to write about: <u>skateboarding on our curb</u>

From *Read and Write Sports: Readers Theatre and Writing Activities for Grades 3–8* by Anastasia Suen. Santa Barbara, CA: Libraries Unlimited. Copyright © 2011.

Name **Tyler**   Date **June 5**

Skateboarding Scene Threes GO Chart

Real life goes on and on but a story starts when something changes. Your readers want to find out how someone solves a problem. Where is that person and what is the problem? Decide on the 3 essential elements of your scene. Use short phrases to record your decisions.

I want to write about: **skateboarding on our curb**

To write a scene, you need 3 things:

a **PERSON:** a skateboarder

in a **PLACE:** at the curb in front of the house

with a **PROBLEM:** with friends who say they can skate better

Name Tyler   Date June 5

Skateboarding Scene Story Boxes (Step 1) GO Chart

Step 1: What happens during your scene? Write a short action phrase in each box.

waxing curb

friends come over

ollie

caveman

50-50 grind

manual

5-0 grind

Name Tyler   Date June 5

Skateboarding Scene Story Boxes (Step 2) GO Chart

Step 1: What happens during your scene? Write a short action phrase in each box.

in front of house skateboard on sidewalk	**waxing curb**	put on helmet sunny afternoon
1st friend skates up 2nd friend comes over	**friends come over**	look at curb bragging starts
I pop my board and ollie ask them to try	**ollie**	1st friend ollies 2nd friend ollies
2nd friend does caveman I try caveman	**caveman**	1st friend does caveman other kids come to watch
1st friend does 50-50 grind 2nd friend does 50-50 grind	**50-50 grind**	I do 50-50 grind neighborhood kids clap
I do manual 1st friend does manual	**manual**	2nd friend does manual neighborhood kids cheer
2nd friend tries 5-0 grind 1st friend tries 5-0 grind	**5-0 grind**	only I can do 5-0 grind! proud!

Step 2: Add 4 details (actions, descriptions, feelings) to each box.

From *Read and Write Sports: Readers Theatre and Writing Activities for Grades 3–8* by Anastasia Suen. Santa Barbara, CA: Libraries Unlimited. Copyright © 2011.

Name Lauren   Date June 8

Skateboarding Moment Mind Map GO Chart

A poem can capture a moment in time. What is happening in this sports moment? Write your sport in the center circle and add details in the smaller circles.

I want to write about this moment in time: __the half pipe__

Name <u>Lauren</u>   Date <u>June 8</u>

Skateboarding Moment 6 Ws GO Chart

Answering the 6 Ws will help you write your sports moment poem.

I want to write about this moment in time: <u>the half pipe</u>

Who is the main character? <u>me</u>

What happens? <u>skateboarding</u>

When does it happen? <u>on the weekend</u>

Where does it happen? <u>at the skatepark</u>

Why does it happen? <u>my turn to skate the half pipe</u>

How does it happen?

   Action: <u>I put my board at the top of the half pipe</u>

   Reaction: <u>I drop in</u>

Name <u>Lauren</u>   Date <u>June 8</u>

Skateboarding Moment Poetry Stretch

Add details to your 6 Ws and stretch your sports moment thoughts into a poem. Write your first draft below.

<u>the half pipe is finally free</u>

<u>I ride over</u>

<u>and stop at the top</u>

<u>I move my back wheels over the edge</u>

<u>and stand on the tail</u>

<u>the board hovers in the air</u>

<u>I stomp on the front of the board</u>

<u>THUMP!</u>

<u>down I go...</u>

Skateboarding Word Search

```
C N P E I L L O Z C O N V O T
I U H Z Z X A W D R O P I N A
X D J G V K N N Y L T O X Y I
K H E L M E T Q Z F I G Q L L
M D A S F E P I P F L A H I O
V G O O F Y F O O T A R B M R
D S K A T E P A R K I X A X F
L H M G B A E S R A D N Y A J
D S K C U R T L C T U N K C C
K Q X C C A V E M A N I I B E
W L E S O N S A L G E T S R B
B A C K S I D E T S L I A R G
C D T G U H K I E R U C C K T
M M Y M S K A T E B O A R D W
S F R O N T S I D E Q Y G R W
```

air	fakie	helmet	skateboard
backside	frontside	manual	skate park
bail	goofyfoot	nose	tail
caveman	grind	ollie	trucks
drop in	half pipe	rails	wax

From *Read and Write Sports: Readers Theatre and Writing Activities for Grades 3–8* by Anastasia Suen. Santa Barbara, CA: Libraries Unlimited. Copyright © 2011.

Skateboarding Crossword Puzzle

ACROSS

2 Scraping the axles on a curb or rail.

5 Front and rear axles with wheels.

6 Skating the board backwards while facing forwards.

7 A trick done with the skater facing the obstacle.

9 A jump done by tapping the tail of the skateboard.

DOWN

1 Riding with all four wheels off the ground.

2 Riding with the right foot forward.

3 A trick done with the skater's back to the obstacle.

4 Front of the skateboard.

8 Back of the skateboard.

Appendix 1

Writing Charts

Name_____ Date _____

Write an Expository Paragraph Chart

1. Select a topic.

2. Think of a question.

3. Find 5 facts that answer your question.

4. Organize your facts.

5. Write about your facts.

Name_____ Date _____

Topic Mind Map GO Chart

Write the name of your sport in the center circle and add details in the smaller circles. This brainstorming will help you figure out a research question. What do you want to know about this sport?

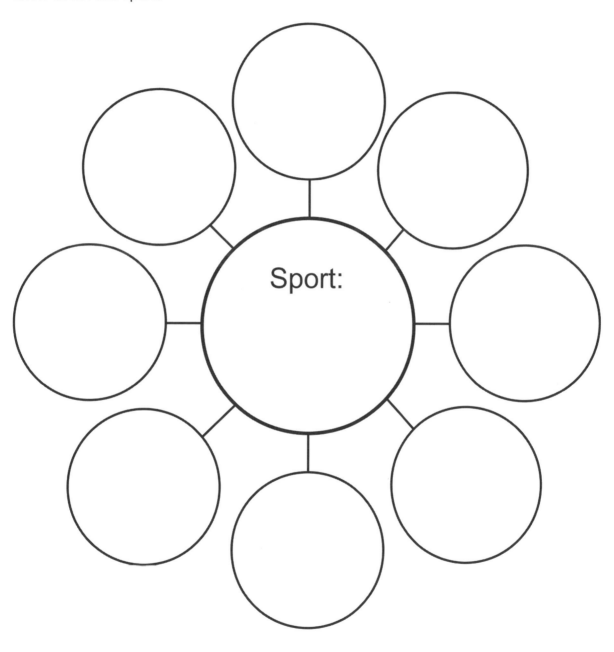

I want to know: _____

Name_____ Date _____

Topic
ISP
GO Chart

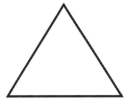

Find the answer to your sports research question with this ISP chart. Use short phrases to record your Information, Source, and Page.

I want to know: _____

I:_____
S:_____
P:_____

I:_____
S:_____
P:_____

I:_____
S:_____
P:_____

I:_____
S:_____
P:_____

I:_____
S:_____
P:_____

Topic Sandwich GO Chart

Organize the information from your ISP chart so you can write your sports paragraph.

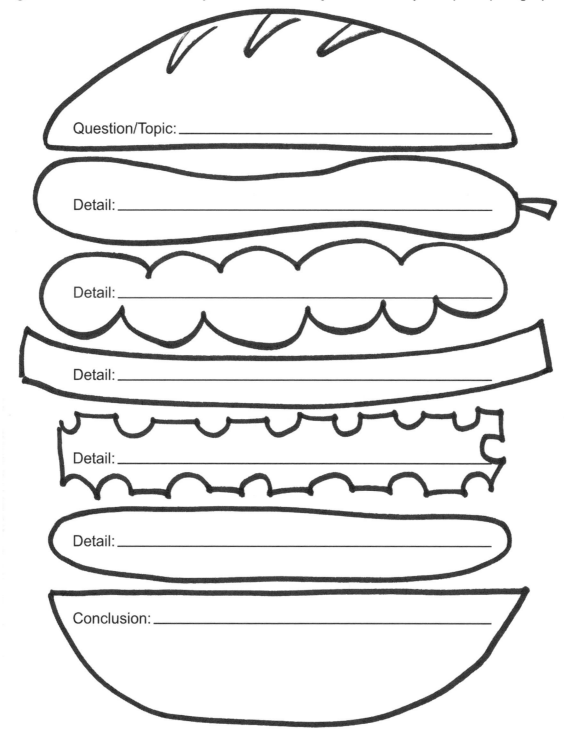

Question/Topic:_____

Detail:_____

Detail:_____

Detail:_____

Detail:_____

Detail:_____

Conclusion:_____

From *Read and Write Sports: Readers Theatre and Writing Activities for Grades 3–8* by Anastasia Suen. Santa Barbara, CA: Libraries Unlimited. Copyright © 2011.

Write a Narrative Scene Chart

1. Make a mind map.

2. Think threes (a person in a place with a problem).

3. Make an action list.

4. Add details.

5. Write your scene.

Name_____ Date_____

Scene Mind Map GO Chart

A scene is a small part of a longer story. It is over in a matter of minutes. What can happen in just a few minutes when you play this sport? Write the sport in the center circle and add details in the smaller circles. This will help you decide what aspect of this sport you can write about today.

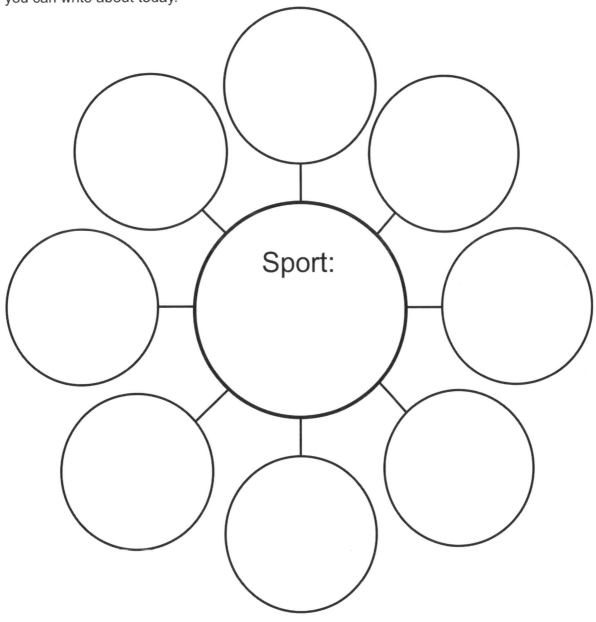

I want to write about:_____

Scene Threes GO Chart

Real life goes on and on but a story starts when something changes. Your readers want to find out how someone solves a problem. Where is that person and what is the problem? Decide on the 3 essential elements of your scene. Use short phrases to record your decisions.

I want to write about:_____

To write a scene, you need 3 things:

a PERSON: _____

in a PLACE: _____

with a PROBLEM: _____

Scene Story Boxes GO Chart

Step 1: What happens during your scene? Write a short action phrase in each box.

Step 2: Add 4 details (actions, descriptions, feelings) to each box.

Write an Action-Reaction Poem Chart

1. Make a mind map.

2. Answer the 6 Ws.

3. Think action-reaction.

4. Add details.

5. Write your poem.

Name_____ Date_____

Moment Mind Map GO Chart

A poem can capture a moment in time. What is happening in this sports moment? Write your sport in the center circle and add details in the smaller circles.

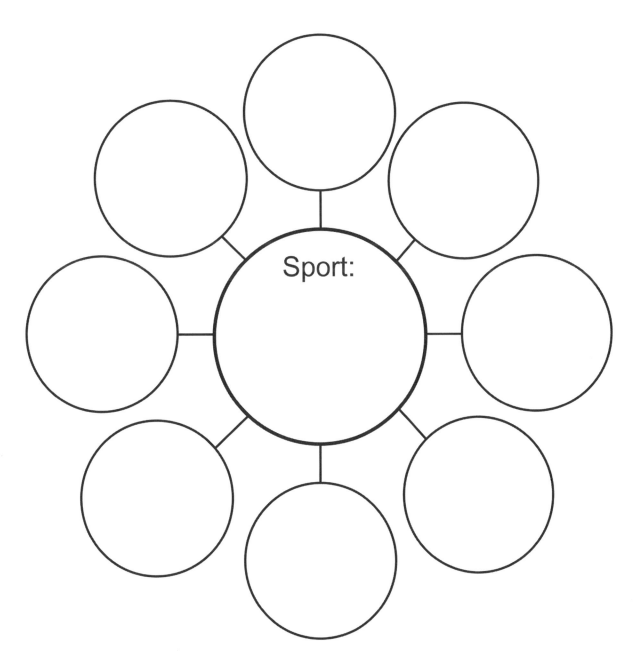

I want to write about this moment in time: _____

From Read and Write Sports: Readers Theatre and Writing Activities for Grades 3–8 by Anastasia Suen. Santa Barbara, CA: Libraries Unlimited. Copyright © 2011.

Name_____ Date _____

Moment 6 Ws GO Chart

Answering the 6 Ws will help you write your sports moment poem.

I want to write about this moment in time: _____

Who is the main character? _____

What happens? _____

When does it happen? _____

Where does it happen?_____

Why does it happen? _____

How does it happen?

    Action: _____

    Reaction: _____

Moment Poetry Stretch

Add details to your 6 Ws and stretch your sports moment thoughts into a poem. Write your first draft below.

_____

_____

_____

_____

_____

_____

_____

_____

_____

_____

_____

_____

_____

_____

_____

_____

_____

_____

_____

_____

_____

_____

Feelings Chart

How does the person feel?

Sad

Happy

Angry

Hurt

Excited

Worried

Bored

Embarrassed

Tired

Name_____ Date_____

Five Senses Chart

Use your five senses:

See

Hear

Touch

Taste

Smell

From *Read and Write Sports: Readers Theatre and Writing Activities for Grades 3–8* by Anastasia Suen. Santa Barbara, CA: Libraries Unlimited. Copyright © 2011.

Simple Proofreading Marks Chart

∧   Insert a word, letter, or phrase

⏗   Delete

☰   Capitalize

/   Change to lowercase

⋏   Insert period

⊙   Insert comma

⌄'   Insert an apostrophe

⌄"   Insert quotations

⋏   Insert space

⌒   Close up space

∽   Switch letters or words

¶   Start a new paragraph

(SP)   Check spelling

⌐   Move right

⌐   Move left

Appendix 2

Puzzle Solutions

Football Word Search Solution

Football Crossword Puzzle Solution

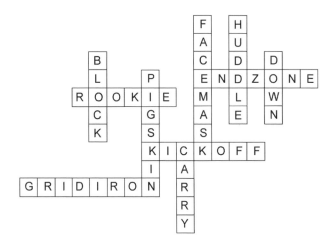

Basketball Word Search Solution

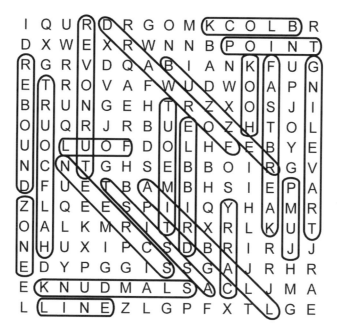

Basketball Crossword Puzzle Solution

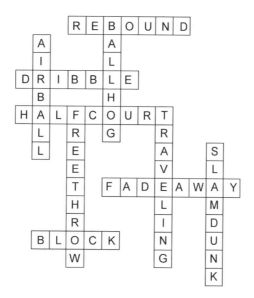

Hockey Word Search Solution

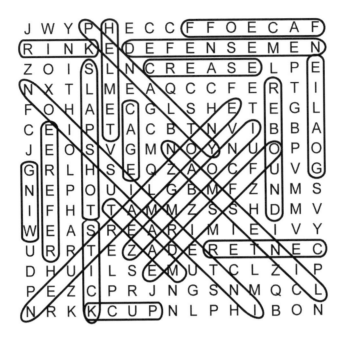

Hockey Crossword Puzzle Solution

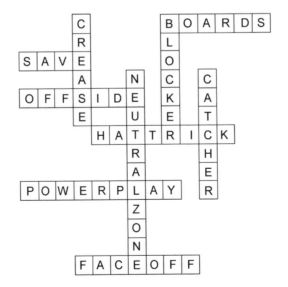

Skating Word Search Solution

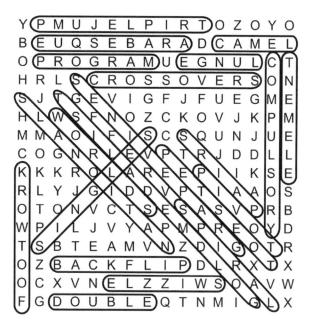

Skating Crossword Puzzle Solution

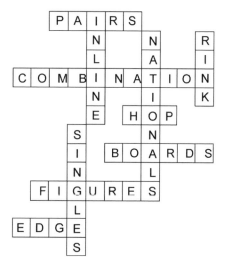

Baseball Word Search Solution

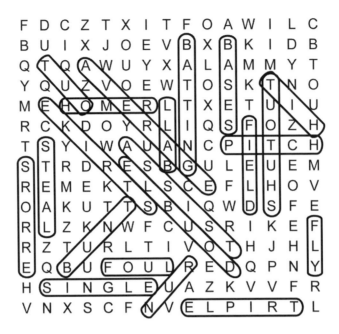

Baseball Crossword Puzzle Solution

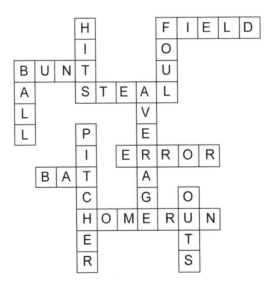

Soccer Word Search Solution

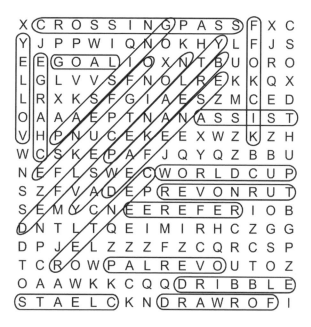

Soccer Crossword Puzzle Solution

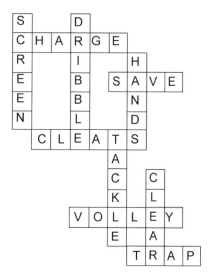

Track Word Search Solution

Track Crossword Puzzle Solution

Gymnastics Word Search Solution

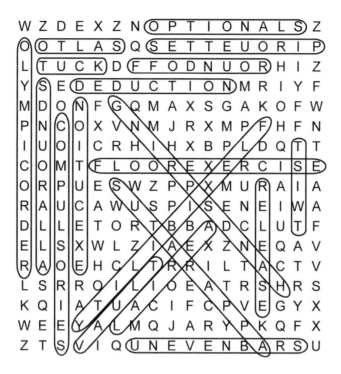

Gymnastics Crossword Puzzle Solution

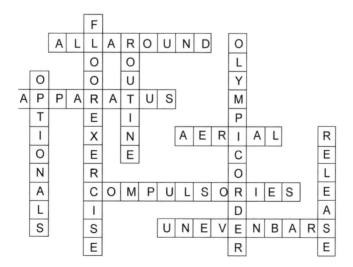

BMX Word Search Solution

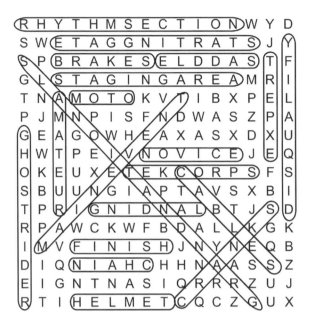

BMX Crossword Puzzle Solution

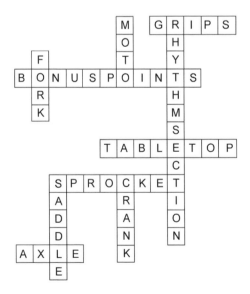

From Read and Write Sports: Readers Theatre and Writing Activities for Grades 3–8
by Anastasia Suen. Santa Barbara, CA: Libraries Unlimited. Copyright © 2011.

Skateboarding Word Search Solution

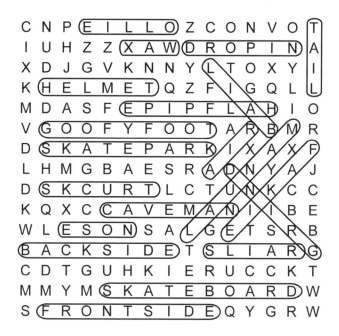

Skateboarding Crossword Puzzle Solution

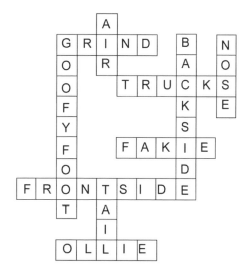

About the Author

ANASTASIA SUEN is the author of over 100 books for children and adults. She has worked as children's literature consultant for Brown Books, Lee and Low Books, National Geographic School Publishers, Rosen Publishing, Sadlier-Oxford, and Scholastic. She writes about new children's books for *Book Links* and on her literacy blogs. A former Kindergarten ESL, first, fifth and sixth grade teacher, she co-taught children's literature at the University of North Texas and conducted teacher inservice for Staff Development for Educators. Today she visits schools to work with teachers and young writers, and teaches writing online and at Southern Methodist University in Dallas, Texas. You will find links to her blogs and more at asuen.com.